RETHINKING ISLAM & THE WEST

RETHINKING ISLAM & THE WEST

A New Narrative for the Age of Crises

Ahmed Paul Keeler

EQUILIBRA

EQUILIBRA PRESS

RETHINKING ISLAM & THE WEST

A New Narrative for the Age of Crises

ISBN: 978-1-9161738-0-4

Equilibra Press
Cambridge
United Kingdom

Book design & typesetting:
New Andalus Productions

Cover image:
Ana Maria Giraldo

Enquiries:
info@equilibrapress.com

CONTENTS

PREFACE

IT IS LATE MARCH, the blackbirds are singing and the cherry trees are in bloom. In this season of renewal, I am putting the finishing touches to a book I began seven years ago. On reaching the age of seventy, I was encouraged to commit to paper ideas and reflections I had shared with friends and colleagues over many years. I was reluctant to write this book, but having been invited by the Centre of Islamic Studies at Cambridge University to become a Visiting Fellow, I was able to test the ideas in lectures and seminars with students and faculty, and this has stimulated me to complete the task.

I grew up under the shadow of the atom bomb. I remember the terror this invoked. We were the first generation to live in the knowledge that we could destroy ourselves and all life on earth. This new power separates our generation from all previous generations. Since the creation of the atom bomb, many other ways of total destruction have been developed. We are now enveloped in an environmental crisis, and the warnings from the scientists of the dangers we face are becoming ever more strident. The impact upon nature of what we have now produced is so great that we are changing the climate. Global warming is an ever-present reminder that something is fundamentally wrong and we are heading towards catastrophe.

But the environmental crisis is not alone. The explosion in the population, financial crises, social and political instability, the growth of mental illness amongst the young, and a host of other problems beset us. Humanity seems to have lost its way. But we are all in this together, we all share this beautiful blue globe which we first saw when its picture was taken from the moon, and its destruction touches each and every one of us.

In our interconnected world whatever happens is instantly known everywhere. We witness the growing tensions and outbreaks of violence between and within different communities and nations as they unfold. In the UK, we are being riven by our separation from the European Community, which has divided our nation and poisoned our politics. A few days ago, fifty worshippers were gunned down when they were at Friday prayer in two Mosques in Christchurch, New Zealand. At the time the massacre was taking place, thousands of children filled the main square of the city. They were demonstrating as part of a world-wide movement against global warming in which the children are castigating the adults for not taking climate change seriously and endangering their future. In England the day after the massacre, the windows of five mosques were smashed, and in Utrecht a Muslim gunned down five people in a tram. The cycle of terror is escalating fuelled by fear, hatred and revenge.

But how different it was some forty years ago! In 1976, a festival celebrating the civilisation of Islam took place in London. The World of Islam Festival, as it was called, included a dozen exhibitions coordinated by the Arts Council of Great Britain and was inaugurated by Her Majesty the Queen. At the time, little was known about Islam and the response to the Festival was overwhelming. The beauty, humanity and intelligence of a civilisation that dominated Afro-Eurasia for more than a thousand years was a revelation, and was warmly received by a public keen to learn about an unfamiliar world. Yet this promising opening was soon eclipsed. Not even three years had passed before a very different image of Islam commanded the public sphere with the Iranian Revolution. This was the beginning of a polarisation between an increasingly distorted image of Islam and the West, that culminated in 9/11 and the War on Terror.

Central to my book is the idea that we are now living in the 'Age of Crises', and have been since the creation of the atom bomb. The ever-present reality that we can destroy ourselves and all life on earth in multiple ways hovers over our existence. In the following pages, the attempt is made to understand how we have arrived in this Age of Crises, and to untangle the confusion and hostility that now exists between Islam and the West.

In order to do this, I am proposing a change of perspective, a different narrative and set of criteria. The narrative which powers the modern world is that of progress and it has gathered up all of history in its wake. Islam and pre-modern cultures and civilisations are viewed through this prism. However, the modern idea of progress belongs uniquely to the West. It makes little sense when applied to Islam and pre-modern societies. I propose in the following pages to replace the criterion of progress with that of balance, a central principle in Islamic civilisation, and indeed an essential precondition for the sustainability of any culture or civilisation. Our Age of Crises can be seen as a result of the loss of balance that has taken place in our modern way of life; the balance between the material and the spiritual, and between ourselves and the environment in which we live.

The book begins with an introduction which sets out the arguments for a new narrative and outlines the criteria of balance that underlie the thesis. The main part of the book comprises seven chapters, six of which encompass themes which are applied firstly to Islam and then to the West. These themes are what we might call key components in the formation and historical development of the two worlds. The final chapter addresses the Age of Crises, and a brief conclusion summarises how Islam and the West are viewed from the perspective of balance. Also included is a glossary of terms and principles that have arisen out of the study, some of which have been newly coined.

My hope is that this comparative analysis makes sense of our Age of Crises, illuminates our understanding of the modern world, and enables us to see Islam and Islamic civilisation in a truer light.

This book has come out of my life experience, and in that journey, so many people have opened my eyes and contributed to my understanding. I want to thank all of them and especially those who have supported, encouraged and engaged in the research, editing and production of this work over the last seven years. Any mistakes or misjudgements are entirely my own.

Cambridge, March 2019

INTRODUCTION

THE POWER OF THE PRESENT NARRATIVE

ISLAM AND THE WEST have been neighbours for 1400 years. The West grew up under the shadow of Islam, and then after the Renaissance, in a dramatic reversal of roles, the West became world conquerors and subdued all other cultures and civilisations, including Islam. This transformation ushered in the modern world, a world unlike any that had existed before. A key development in this transformation took place when, during the Enlightenment, a narrative was produced which introduced the idea of human progress. This was a revolutionary concept that would replace the Christian narrative of salvation.

This new narrative saw the Christian millennium as a dark age of ignorance and superstition. It became known as the Medieval or Middle Ages, a period between the illumination of the ancients and the light of the modern world. Later, Islam was introduced into this narrative by giving it a 'golden age' during Europe's Dark Ages, a time when it kept alight the torch of Greek and Roman knowledge. It was said that, having passed the torch to the Europeans, who then accelerated into their dynamic arc of progress, the Muslims went into a deep decline and stagnation. The world of Islam is now part of a developing world that is having to catch up with the West. In brief, the narrative tells of the triumph of the West and how the rest were left behind, including Islam.

The philosophers and thinkers of the 18th and 19th centuries who were responsible for developing the modern idea of progress, approached its unfolding in very different ways. Immanuel Kant saw progress as 'man's emergence from his self-incurred immaturity.' For Hegel, the constant convulsions and revolutions in modern European history entail that it is the European alone who embodies freedom and progress. According to his view, when a political and social state of affairs (thesis) is rocked by conflict and opposition (antithesis), revolution brings about human freedom and greater societal progress (synthesis). Hegel believed that periods of happiness are empty pages in history, times when the antithesis is missing, with the result that 'the history of China has shown no development. China and India, as it were, lie outside the course of world history.' Karl Marx believed that on their road to progress, human societies must pass through primitive communism, slave societies, feudalism, capitalism and socialism before culminating in fully-fledged communism. August Comte taught that the scientific method was the only guarantor of knowledge and had replaced metaphysics in man's social evolution. In his law of human progress, Comte taught that human societies must pass through three stages: the theological, the metaphysical and the positive or scientific. Herbert Spencer, following in the steps of Darwin, believed that progress was not an accident, but a necessity; humanity must evolve to become perfect. This perfection, however, was only available to Europeans, since the physical characteristics typical of progress are 'stronger in the European than in the savage'. It was not Darwin but Spencer, who coined the term 'survival of the fittest'.

The narrative of progress is deeply embedded in our consciousness. It informs our language, has moulded the way we think, and is the global narrative which powers the modern world. In our contemporary culture, there is a sharp demarcation between positive words such as 'innovation', 'development', 'change', 'ground-breaking' and 'cutting-edge', and those that carry a negative connotation, like 'Dark Ages', 'medieval', 'reactionary' and 'backward-looking'.

What would appear to be the indisputable achievement of modernity is clearly articulated by the Australian economist Wolfgang Kasper:

> Against the experience of long-term stagnation and misery, the record of growing prosperity over the past two centuries and, in particular, the last fifty years, is astounding.

Anthony Burton in *The Rise and Fall of King Cotton* makes the case that the Industrial Revolution rescued humanity from a past of hardship and starvation:

> The old world was one that was primarily concerned with keeping alive. It was an agricultural society, forever balanced on the edge of subsistence which marks off comfort from starvation. The new world is dynamic, geared to the notion of continuous economic growth. Very few would argue that starvation is preferable to comfort, nor could they argue that the change from one condition to the other would have been possible without industrialisation. So, it should logically follow that industrialisation is an essential stage through which man must pass if he is to enjoy a decent life.

The unquestioning belief in human progress informs politics across the world, from the late Senator John McCain's statement, 'America's greatest strength has always been its hopeful vision of human progress', to that of the Chinese premier, Li Keqiang, 'Change calls for innovation, and innovation leads to progress.'

However, cracks in this supremely powerful edifice are now appearing. Whilst the theory of human progress has been challenged by philosophers and thinkers for more than a hundred years, unease concerning it is now reaching the multitude. The endless reliving of the terrible world wars of the 20th century in books, TV documentaries and Hollywood films, in an attempt to understand the horrors that were committed, undermines the very idea of human progress. The cosmologist, Lawrence M Krauss tried to counter the terrifying views of the future presented in films like *Mad Max*, *Blade Runner* and *The Matrix* when he stated:

> Often, too often, it seems to me, in science fiction there's a dystopic view of the future, that science makes the world a worse place. Science has made the world a much better place. People live much happier lives, much healthier lives on the whole and much longer because of science.

Meanwhile, capitalism, the bastion of progress, is under siege in the media and on the streets. The present British Prime Minister Theresa May recently stated in its defence:

> A free market economy, operating under the right rules and regulations, is the greatest agent of collective human progress ever created. It was this new combination which led societies out of darkness and stagnation into the light of the modern age.

In this statement, Theresa May could not have more clearly articulated the false premise that underpins the theory of progress, namely, the great modern fallacy that humanity has been rescued from a past of misery, stagnation and poverty and brought into the light of the modern age. The modern narrative tells the story of how the Industrial Revolution took place in England because of particular social, economic and material advantages that England enjoyed. England took the leap forward into a world of plenty and improvement, leaving behind the struggle for survival; Europe followed and now the rest of the world is in the process of catching up.

The truth is rather that a world of many cultures and civilisations that had accumulated vast knowledge of how to live sustainably and in balance with the natural world, was destroyed and re-ordered to serve the industrial system. This was a world of bio-diversity and cultural-diversity, whose societies were organised for the benefit of their people, had developed highly sophisticated arts and sciences to support their ways of life, and were devoted to their various religious practices. The impoverishment which took place during the 19th Century, with its plantations, mines and sweatshops, was the creation of the Europeans, and it was out of this destruction of living cultures and civilisations that the Industrial Revolution was born and the modern world came into being.

Fortunately, the Europeans gathered together in their libraries and museums all the evidence required to piece together what actually happened, and living remnants of those worlds are still with us. The true horror of what occurred through the building, maintaining and dissolution of the European empires is only now coming to light. The generations born after they came to an end are not trapped in the myths that were woven into the narratives of empire, and are fast unravelling them. To see the film *The Four Feathers*, set during the 19th century British colonial war in the Sudan and released in 1938, is to witness a completely different mentality from that of today. The film presents the British as men of boundless honour, loyalty and courage, and the Sudanese warriors are there simply to be mown down by superior weaponry, as were the 'Red Indians' in cowboy films that were so popular in the 1940s and 50s.

Scholars and journalists, who often witness first-hand the sufferings and dislocation of the post-colonial world we live in, are producing well-researched studies of every aspect of the past that can be accessed through the meticulous records that the Europeans maintained. At the same time, in the post-colonial world, young scholars, trained in the Western academic system of forensic research, are trawling through the records, trying to piece together what actually happened during the period of the European empires.

So many myths are being exploded. One, in which we British pride ourselves, is the abolition of slavery. The general understanding is that slavery was abolished through the heroic efforts of William Wilberforce in 1807. In fact, in that year only the trade was abolished. It was not until 1834 that slavery itself was abolished. There is no doubt that William Wilberforce and others laboured in a noble cause. However, a team of scholars from University College London have discovered evidence that has cast a very different light on the matter. They came across hundreds of albums containing the records of compensation paid to the slave owners for the release of their slaves. The government paid out what in today's money would be around £17 billion to 46,000 people who had shares in the ownership of 800,000 slaves in the West Indies. The slaves were not released immediately but had to work a further transition period. Everything was done for the benefit of the slave owners; the slaves received nothing and were mostly re-employed as cheap labour.

However, those working in the sugar plantations, which were death traps, left as soon as they were able. The author of *Coolie Odyssey*, David Dabydeen, whose ancestors ended up in the West Indies as indentured labourers, takes up the story of what happened next. With the loss of their slaves, the sugar plantation owners petitioned the British government to pass a law to allow indentured labour. This was vigorously opposed by the Foreign Secretary, Lord John Russell, who saw it as slavery under another guise, but the law was passed owing to the powerful lobbying of the plantation owners. There followed 80 years of a system, little better than slavery, in which one and a half million Indians, impoverished by British policies regarding their rural environment, were shipped to different parts of the Empire to toil in British-owned plantations and mines. The infamous practice only came to an end in 1917 when Gandhi led a campaign for its abolition whilst he was practising as a lawyer in South Africa.

It is, however, the post-modern philosophers, such as Foucault, Derrida and Butler, who express the ultimate disillusion with modernity and are delivering the death blow to the idea of progress. Their ideas are riding high in the universities of the West and are seeping into the mainstream of society. Their philosophy is challenging hierarchy and reducing everything to a state of relativity. It is a critique that offers little to humanity and is, in fact, the last and closing manifestation of the West's downward trajectory.

But what of the other conquest undertaken by European civilisation, namely, the conquest of nature? This is proving to be a pyrrhic victory. There is no question that we have achieved much of what the 16th century natural philosopher Francis Bacon aspired to in 'wringing from nature her secrets and exploiting her powers'. However, in so doing, we have created an environmental crisis that threatens to destroy us. Modern man is being enveloped by multiple, exponential and escalating crises of unprecedented, unimaginable scale.

THE AGE OF CRISES

THE ATOM BOMB launched humanity into a new age; one in which for the first time we could envisage the destruction of life on earth by our own hand. Since the splitting of the atom, many other means to bring about total destruction have been devised in the laboratories of the scientists; yet it is they who are warning us that we are now standing on the threshold of global annihilation. In what follows, I have outlined some of the landmarks in the unfolding of the crises.

In 1947, *The Bulletin of the Atomic Scientists* set up the Doomsday Clock. The clock was intended to represent an analogy for the threat of global nuclear war. Since

2007, it has also reflected climate change, and new developments in the life sciences and technology that could inflict irrevocable harm on humanity. On the clock, the hypothetical global catastrophe is presented as 'midnight' and *The Bulletin*'s opinion on how close the world is to a global catastrophe as the number of minutes to midnight. Its original setting in 1947 was seven minutes to midnight. It has been set backward and forward 23 times since then, the smallest-ever number of minutes to midnight being two; this occurred in 1953 and in January 2018, due to 'the looming threats of nuclear war and climate change'. As of January 2019, the clock still stands at two minutes to twelve.

In 1962, Rachel Carson's book *Silent Spring* was published in America, in which she warned against the dangers of the pesticide DDT. The book was met with fierce opposition from chemical companies. One spokesman stated, 'Miss Carson claims that the balance of nature is a major force in the survival of man, whereas the modern chemist, the modern biologist, the modern scientist believes that man is steadily controlling nature.' Her book sold half a million copies in six months, and her case was so well argued, striking a nerve in popular consciousness, that it spurred a reversal in national pesticide policy, led to a nationwide ban on DDT for agricultural uses, and inspired an environmental movement that led to the creation of the U.S Environmental Protection Agency. The book had a global impact, bringing to the world's attention the dangers of chemical agriculture and the futility of the war against bugs, which would simply lead to their mutating and becoming ever more dangerous.

However, scientists are telling us that spring is now silent across most of the developed agricultural lands. The naturalist and TV presenter Chris Packham, in a deep analysis of the rapid disappearance of flora and fauna in the UK concluded, 'Our generation is presiding over an ecological apocalypse and we've somehow or other normalised it.' German scientists are warning of 'ecological Armageddon' as a recent study shows that three-quarters of flying insects in nature reserves across Germany have vanished in the last 25 years. The California almond crop is pollinated by bees that are being shipped thousands of miles across America on trucks. Report after report carries the same message: we are destroying the eco-system on which we depend.

In 1972, *The Limits to Growth* was published by the Club of Rome. For the first time, this report brought to the attention of a global public the contradiction between exponential economic and population growth on the one hand, and a finite world on the other.

In 2008, the world financial system came perilously close to collapse. It began in 2007 with a crisis in the sub-prime mortgage market in the United States, and developed into a full-blown international banking crisis. Excessive risk-taking by banks helped to magnify the financial impact globally. Massive bail-outs of financial institutions and other palliative monetary and fiscal policies were employed by governments. Whilst the bankers came out of the crisis which they had caused unscathed, millions of ordinary people's livelihoods were destroyed. William White, the central banker who famously predicted the crisis of 2008, has warned that 'the world is facing a new crisis caused by an explosion of debt.' Many economists now see as inevitable the collapse of the modern financial system that has lost touch with reality. Global growth is now fuelled by governments going deeper and deeper into debt, made possible by the creation of money out of thin air. The banks were bailed out by governments, but who, the economists ask, will bail out the governments?

In 2009, Sir John Beddington, Chief Scientific Adviser to the UK Government, warned of a perfect storm on the horizon:

> It is predicted that by 2030 the world will need to produce 50% more food and energy, together with 30% more available fresh water, whilst mitigating and adapting to climate change. This threatens to create a 'perfect storm' of global events.

In 2012, responding to the deepening environmental and other crises, Sir Martin Rees, the Astronomer Royal, co-founded at Cambridge University the Centre for the Study of Existential Risks. The Centre is dedicated to the study and mitigation of risks that could lead to human extinction or civilisational collapse. Their research focuses on biological risks, environmental risks, risks from artificial intelligence, and how to manage extreme technological risk in general.

In 2017, Dame Sally Davies, Chief Medical Officer for England, was so alarmed by the build-up of resistance to antibiotics, that she warned we faced a 'post antibiotic holocaust' if we continued along this trajectory. She stated, 'Super bugs will kill us before climate change'.

But it is global warming that has tipped the balance, and is now providing a consensus among scientists that it is our way of life that is the root cause of the phenomenon. Something is fundamentally wrong with the way we are living on earth. Although climate change had been discussed within the scientific community for decades, it was in 1976 with the Russian climatologist Mikhail Budyko's statement 'a global warming up has started', that it was reported more widely. It took a decade for the international community to become fully engaged, and then the ponderous global institutions were mobilised and new bodies formed to address the crisis. In 1988, the Inter-governmental Panel on

Climate Change (IPCC) was jointly established by the World Meteorological Organization (WMO) and the United Nations Environment Programme (UNEP), and later endorsed by the United Nations General Assembly. The IPCC produces reports that support the United Nations Framework Convention on Climate Change (UNFCCC), the main international treaty. The objective of the UNFCCC is to 'stabilize greenhouse gas concentrations in the atmosphere at a level that would prevent dangerous anthropogenic (human-induced) interference with the climate system'. Now there are thousands of scientists world-wide, who are engaged in the study of climate change and global warming. Their warnings are becoming ever more urgent, but the temperature continues to rise. In its latest report the WMO states:

> The concentrations of key gases in the atmosphere that are driving up global temperatures reached a new high in 2017 and there is no sign of reversal in this rising trend.

UN Secretary General Antonio Guterres reported in September 2018:

> Climate change is moving faster than we are … if the world doesn't change course by 2020, we run the risk of runaway climate change … we are careering towards the edge of the abyss.

Many scientists cannot see us surviving the crises, including the late Professor Stephen Hawking, who spent the last years of his life researching space travel to take us to other solar systems. In his final book, *Brief Answers to the Big Questions*, he stated:

> We have given the planet a disastrous gift of climate change, rising temperatures, reduction of the polar ice caps, deforestation and decimation of animal species; we are running out of space; the only places to go to are other worlds. It is time to explore other solar systems; spreading out may be the only thing that saves us from ourselves.

We have now travelled far into the Age of Crises and ironically it is the scientists, out of whose laboratories the crises have emerged, that are daily warning us of the perils we face. We are also being educated concerning the proliferation of natural disasters that are being exacerbated by global warming, such as the increase in the severity and frequency of hurricanes and, with the rise of sea levels, the increased damage caused by inundations to coastal and island communities.

Lawrence M Krauss demonstrated the fragility of the artificial world we have created when he surmised that a giant solar flare could destroy the information fabric of the world and, with it, modern civilisation would collapse. With all of these man-made threats joining traditional fears of the four horsemen of the apocalypse – pestilence, war, famine and death – it is no wonder there is political and social unrest and an alarming increase in mental illness amongst the young.

But there is another fear that has emerged out of the chaos of the Age of Crises; this is what has become known as Islamic terrorism, a phenomenon replicating modernist ideologies and subverting the traditional patterns of Islam. Beginning in the late 1970's it reached a crescendo with the destruction of the World Trade Centre in New York on 11 September 2001. For the USA it was seen as the deadliest event since Pearl Harbour and ushered in 'the war on terror', an expression first used by George W Bush. This war, which now engages many nations around the world against an enemy that has no territorial base, has led to a transformation in homeland defence and the conduct of warfare. Muslims are watching in horror as a newly-created sect, driven by rage and revenge, is perpetuating acts of indescribable cruelty in the name of Islam – an ignorant sect that is breaking the fundamental tenets of Islam in a vain and ludicrous quest for universal hegemony, a sect that is making the world hate and despise their religion. The ill-conceived Iraq war escalated the terrorism and has brought chaos to the Middle East, resulting in the greatest displacement of people since World War II.

A West that is losing confidence in its identity sees Islam as a cultural threat and is pulling up the drawbridge. Fortress Europe and America are attempting to stem the flow of migrants, many of whom are Muslims seeking shelter from the storm. Nationalism and the extreme right, which have such a terrible and recent history in Europe, are on the rise. The stage is becoming perilously set for the Muslim to become the scape-goat for a western world in crisis.

Those wishing to defend Islam, both westerners and Muslims, invoke the 'Golden Age of Islam' and the contribution that Muslims made during the European Dark Ages to the creation of the Modern World. But this opens the door to detractors, who ask 'What have they contributed since?' Amongst these is the philosopher Sir Roger Scruton, who in his introduction to Robert R Reilly's book *The Closing of the Muslim Mind*, writes, 'If Reilly is right, as he surely is … this failure … is the effect of an act of cultural and intellectual suicide, which occurred eight centuries ago.' And herein lies the problem of the Golden Age thesis, for although it appears to be complimentary, in fact, it turns Islam into a bit-player in the Western narrative of progress.

This narrative has been so powerful for so long that educated Muslims have completely bought into it, accepting the idea that Islam has become a tributary feeding into the mainstream of modern civilisation. Its value is now judged purely in terms of what Europe received from it. However, I shall argue that the

Golden Age thesis shuts out the understanding of what actually happened, and has caused great confusion in the Muslim mind. Practically everything we know about Islam has been projected through the lens of progress, which serves only to distort and disfigure its true nature, and draw the Muslims into a state of deepening crisis.

The multiple and escalating crises that encompass us are of a scale that goes beyond anything that humanity has ever faced. Scientists are having to resort to biblical terms such as 'apocalypse' and 'Armageddon' in their attempts to communicate the imminent dangers threatening us. But the modern world doggedly continues along its trajectory, because it knows no other way. So much has been invested in the construction of this artificial world. Like a cancer, it is growing on a host that is dying; it only knows how to grow and will go on growing until its host can no longer support it. Modern man is trapped in a system that is failing. Unable to see beyond the walls that imprison him, he clings on in the vain hope that somehow the multiplying crises will be solved by the very science and technology that is causing the destruction in the first place.

The theory of progress has run its course and as Adam Curtis says at the end of his thought-provoking documentary *Bitter Lake*, 'What is needed is a new story and one that we can believe in'.

MĪZĀN AND THE PERSPECTIVE OF BALANCE

IN LOOKING FOR a new story, a narrative which can make more sense of our past and the situation in which we now find ourselves, a criterion needs to be found in place of that of progress, and I believe this to be the criterion of balance. Few would argue with the idea that humanity is out of balance with the natural world and that this disequilibrium has now reached a critical stage. Balance is manifested in many ways within cultures and civilisations, and if things are out of balance, sooner or later they fall apart. In pre-modern cultures, this balance has been understood to include the balance between the heavenly, human and earthly dimensions of existence. The principle of balance was at the heart of both Confucian China and Islam, and explains the stability and longevity of their civilisations.

In this comparative study of Islam and the West, I shall draw on the Islamic articulation of the concept of balance, represented by the Arabic term *mīzān*, which can be translated as balance, justice, measure, harmony or, indeed, weighing scales. It is a term which contains a spiritual dimension that is not conveyed by our secular understanding of balance. In what follows, I shall use the two words *mīzān* and balance interchangeably, with an awareness of the enhanced meaning contained in the Arabic.

The primacy of *mīzān* and some dimensions of its meaning are presented in the 55th chapter or sura of the Qur'an, Al-Rahmān (The All-Merciful):

> *He raised the heavens and set up everything in balance (mīzān) so that you should not transgress the balance (mīzān). Therefore, maintain just measure and do not fall short in the balance (mīzān).* (Qur'an 55:7-9)

Throughout the following chapters, three fundamental triads, in which the maintenance of balance is essential, will be woven into the fabric of the narrative as it unfolds.

The first is what I have called the 'ontological triad'. Before modernity, all civilisations believed in a sacred origin for their worlds, and in the relationship that had to be maintained between the unseen, the human and the material realms. Christianity and Islam shared an understanding of these realms. We shall see that Islamic civilisation retained the balance and hierarchy within these ontological levels, remaining within the confines of the triad. In the West, however, the collapse of Christendom eventually led to a loss of belief in, and knowledge of, the spiritual realm. This loss of relationship with the unseen made it impossible for ethics and morality to be objectively rooted, or for the integrity of nature to be fully recognized outside of human use and exploitation. We shall see how the breakdown of the hierarchy and balance required within the ontological triad has led to our age of crises.

The second formulation is what I have defined as the 'vocational triad'. The roles of scholars and priests, warriors and rulers, merchants and craftsmen are archetypal, and the relationship between them helps define the character of civilisations. We shall see how in Islam a state of balance, interdependence and fluidity was established between the vocations, creating a stable and sustainable civilisation.

A very different unfolding took place in the West. For a thousand years, Christianity provided a spiritual culture that was intense and single-minded in its vertical aspiration and overwhelmingly dominated by the priest – the Gothic cathedral is the perfect manifestation of this heavenly quest. With the Renaissance, the warrior hero replaced the saint at the apex of society, humanism was born and monarchs became absolute, with the classical palace replacing the Gothic cathedral. The French and American revolutions against the tyranny of monarchs and the fanaticism of the churches, and the Industrial Revolution, brought the merchant, craftsman and natural philosopher into power, and the machine world we now inhabit was their creation. The West has proceeded from intense spirituality through humanism to the all-encompassing materiality that now surrounds us. We shall see how each vocation in the West created its own world, and how, what I call the 'open-plan brain' of the modern, contains all three worlds, somehow co-existing together, but in a permanent state of conflict and contradiction.

Lastly, we have the Platonic triad. Plato formulated the principle of the need to balance three faculties within the human being, namely, those of intellect, anger and desire – a principle that was adopted and developed by both Christianity and Islam. If intellect controls anger and desire, there is peace and harmony; if anger or desire control intellect, conflict and chaos ensue. This triad relates to the individual soul and is also mirrored in the vocational triad, with intellect corresponding to the scholar, anger to the warrior and desire to the merchant. The Platonic triad has remained fundamental to Islam and Christianity, being central to the disciplining of the soul. However, the reign of the warrior in the West unleashed a flood of violence and anger upon the world, and this was joined by the unfettering of desire with the ascendancy of the merchant, finally leading to the overturning of Christian morality.

Appearing within the fabric of the chapters are the pairs, the natural balance between heaven and earth, night and day, inner and outer, male and female and other pairs that encompass our existence.

We have also introduced the term 'dynamic equilibrium', which comes from the material sciences and is defined as 'a state of balance between continuing processes,' or 'a system in a steady state', to describe the dynamic which maintains *mīzān* or balance. It is the incapacity to understand this dynamic that has led the modern to regard pre-modern, traditional cultures and civilisations as static and stagnant. Each traditional civilisation contains a sacred centre which is unchanging, and it is this sacred centre that contains its life-force. When it is compromised, the civilisation runs down. Uniquely, modernity has dispensed with a sacred centre and has turned perpetual change into its dynamic.

Islamic civilisation has an incredibly powerful sacred centre. Throughout Islamic history, whatever forces caused disruption for a time, the unchanging core has always brought the civilisation back into a state of balance and stability. This unchanging and constant reality is centred on the Revelation of the Qur'an and the life of the Prophet, and emanating from these, the Five Pillars of Islam. The establishment of all of this belonged to the twenty-three years of the Prophetic mission and has remained constant and unchanged, until today.

The *mīzān* perspective embodies two important principles: the 'mereological' and the 'chthonic'. The mereological principle states that 'the whole can contain the part, but the part cannot contain the whole'. This principle, I argue, helps to explain the historical success of Islamic civilisation, as well as the aberrational nature of modernity. The chthonic principle states that 'the deeper you go into matter, the greater the forces that are released'; we see the reality of this principle being played out today in the laboratories of scientists.

In the chapters which follow, we shall see how, when Islam and the West are viewed through the lens of *mīzān* or balance, an entirely different story unfolds: the Western trajectory can be seen to lead inexorably to the Age of Crises, whilst a new understanding of Islam and its civilisation emerges.

1

SOVEREIGNTY

ISLAM

WHAT HAS BEEN defined above as the 'ontological triad' depends on the maintenance within a civilisation of balance in the essential relationship between three levels of existence, those of the unseen, the human and the natural world. In Islam, the *mīzān* is predicated on upholding the authority and sovereignty of God as Creator and Ruler of the universe. From the *mīzān* perspective, we are not talking about a balance between equals; rather it is through the sovereignty of God that balance and harmony is maintained in the created world.

In the Qur'an, the Creator's authority is unequivocally stated in this verse from the sura entitled al-Mulk ('Sovereignty' or 'Dominion'):

> *Blessed is He in whose hand is the dominion, and He has power over all things.* (Qur'an 67:1)

This is a theme that is stated time and time again in the Qur'an, reminding humanity of the divine omnipotence. The all-encompassing power of God over His creation is further described in the Throne verse, which according to a saying of the Prophet Muhammad is the greatest verse in the Qur'an:

> *In the name of God, the Beneficent, the Merciful.*
> *God! There is no god but He, the Living, the Self-subsisting.*
> *Neither slumber nor sleep overtakes Him.*
> *To Him belongs all that is in the heavens and the earth.*
> *Who is there that shall intercede with Him save by His leave?*
> *He knows what is before them and what is behind them.*
> *And they encompass nothing of His knowledge, save that which He wills.*
> *His throne extends over the heavens and the earth,*
> *The preserving of them wearies Him not,*
> *He is the Sublime, the Tremendous.* (Qur'an 2:255)

The human response to God's absolute and all-encompassing sovereignty is to glorify and worship Him.

> *And We sent no messenger before you but that We revealed to him, 'There is no god save Me, so worship Me'.* (Qur'an, 21:25)

But the human being has been granted the special honour among creatures of being the vicegerent, successor, or representative (*khalīfa*) of God on earth:

> *And He it is who has made you successors in the earth and has raised some of you above others in degrees, so that He may try you in what He has given you.* (Qur'an, 6:165)

Moreover, the Qur'an repeatedly states that God has placed all that is in heaven and on earth at mankind's disposal. However, with this privilege come responsibilities. Firstly, as vicegerent, it is the unique function and duty of human beings that they should know and recognize the Creator through the signs of His creation, as well as showing gratitude for His bounty:

> *...He produces crops for you, and olives, date-palms, grapes and every kind of fruit; surely in this is a sign for people who give thought.*
>
> *He has made subject to you the night and the day; the sun and the moon; and the stars are in subjection by His command. Surely in this are signs for people who use their intellect.*

> *It is He who has made the sea subject, that you may eat from it fresh meat, and bring forth from it ornaments which you wear; and you see the ships cleaving through it, that you may seek of His bounty, and that you may be grateful.* (Qur'an, 16: 11, 12 and 14)

Secondly, human beings have a duty to respect other creatures and take care of the earth:

> *No creature is there crawling on the earth, no bird flying with its wings, but they are nations like yourselves.* (Qur'an, 6:38)

> *...Do not walk in the earth exultantly; God does not love anyone who is proud and boastful.* (Qur'an, 31:18)

> *...Do not be wasteful, for He does not love those who are wasteful.* (Qur'an, 6:141).

Thirdly, the function of vicegerent involves the upholding of justice and virtuous conduct, as in the following words, addressed to the prophet David:

> *...We have indeed made you a vicegerent on the earth; so judge justly between people and do not follow desire that it then lead you astray from the way of God.* (Qur'an, 38:26)

Thus we see that human vicegerency involves a duty towards God, to the creation, and to fellow human beings. But fulfilment of this threefold responsibility depends upon the maintenance of a balance within the human being of the three Platonic capacities that were mentioned above, those of intellect, anger and desire. This principle is clearly expounded in the 13th century Qur'an commentary of Nāsir al-Dīn al-Baydāwī, entitled *Anwār al-tanzīl wa-asrār al-ta'wīl* ('Lights of Revelation and Mysteries of Interpretation'), in the context of verse 30 of Sura al-Baqara:

> *And when your Lord said to the angels, 'I am appointing on earth a vicegerent'. They said: 'Will You place therein one who will make mischief there and shed blood whilst we celebrate Your praises and glorify Your holy name?' He said: 'I know what you know not.'* (Qur'an, 2:30).

Explaining the angels' objection and God's response, Baydāwī states:

> Man possesses three faculties, that are each pivotal to his life situation, those of desire and anger, which can lead to corruption and the shedding of blood, and the intellectual faculty, which calls him to knowledge and obedience … the compound of these faculties yields … the ability to encompass all things and worlds, the origination of arts and sciences, and the drawing out of the positive characteristics of all existent things, from potential to actuality, which is the purpose of the appointment of the vicegerent.

When people are taken over by desire, as we saw from the words addressed to the prophet David in the verse cited above, they will be led from the way of God. In another verse, the dire consequences of being dominated by desire are described:

> *Have you then seen him who has taken as his god his [own] desire, and whom God has knowingly led astray? He has set a seal upon his hearing and his heart, and placed a covering over his sight. So who will guide him after God? Will you not then take heed?* (Qur'an 45:23)

Just as there needs to be a hierarchy in the maintenance of order within the human being, so it is within human society. Several verses in the Qur'an enunciate the divinely-ordained hierarchy among people:

> *We raise in degree whomever We will: but over each one endued with knowledge is one more knowing.* (Qur'an, 12:76)

> *...[He] has raised some of you above others in degrees, so that He may try you in what He has given you.* (Qur'an, 6:165).

But order and balance in society require the existence of a ruler. Sovereignty (*mulk*) is shown in the Qur'an to be ordained and bestowed by God; it was granted to the prophets David and Solomon, and to Saul despite the objections of his people:

> *Then their prophet said to them, 'Verily God has raised up Saul for you as king'. They said, 'How can he be king over us when we have better right than he to kingship, and*

> *he has not been given wealth in abundance?' He said, 'God has chosen him over you and has increased him greatly in wisdom and stature. God gives the kingship to whom He wills; and God is All-embracing, All-knowing'.* (Qur'an, 2:247)

The principle of divine sanction is included in the term 'Sultan' that was later applied to rulers. The Arabic word *sulṭān* has the meaning of 'delegated power' and also of 'permission'. Order in society requires not only that there be some who are granted authority over others, but the compliance of those who are under their sovereignty. Believers are exhorted to:

> *Obey God and obey the Messenger and those in authority among you.* (Qur'an, 4:59)

Nonetheless, the Western idea of the oriental despot, which surfaced during the Enlightenment and has remained in the Western imagination since, is very far from the reality of the power that Muslim rulers actually wielded, and in fact reflects the despotic power of the absolute monarchs of Europe. The sultan's authority was circumscribed by clearly defined norms within society. Rulers, like everyone else, were subject to the sharia, which was under the authority of the scholar. Rulers had command over their courts and the appointment of judges and other key functionaries, such as market inspectors and tax collectors. However, the administration of justice was the preserve of the scholar. Amongst the ruler's functions was the protection of his realm so that the Islamic way of life could be lived in peace, keeping open the routes for the pilgrims and traders, and supporting the scholars and craftsmen responsible for the intellectual and material domains of the world under his jurisdiction. As a patron, he would protect orphans and the poor, and endow mosques, colleges, hospitals and other charitable institutions. If he was a wise ruler he would be remembered with gratitude for generations, if bad, he would be suffered in patience, with the knowledge that he would pass away in time, and if God so willed He would provide a better ruler in his place.

The scholars' understanding of the character and role of the ruler is clearly enunciated in Saʿd al-Dīn al-Taftāzānī's great *kalām* summa, *Sharh al-Maqāsid* ('The Commentary on the Objectives'):

> The Muslims require a political leader who actualises practice of the religion, establishes the *Sunna*, gives justice to the oppressed and fulfils the rights of all. He must be of responsible age, a Muslim, morally upright, free, male, diligent, courageous, possessed of his own point of view, and able to effect that which he chooses to do.

However, the absolute power of God and the ephemeral nature of the power of earthly rulers is unequivocally stated in the Qur'an:

Say: 'O God, Master of the Kingdom, You give sovereignty to whomever You will, and strip away sovereignty from whomever You will. You exalt whomever You will, and You abase whomever You will; in Your hand is all good. You have power over all things.' (Qur'an, 3:26)

THE WEST

IN CHRISTIANITY, as in Islam, God's sovereignty over His creation is absolute:

Great is our Lord and mighty in power; his understanding has no limit (Psalm 147:5)

Yours, Lord, is the greatness and the power and the glory and the majesty and the splendour, for everything in heaven and earth is yours. Yours, Lord, is the kingdom; you are exalted as head over all. Wealth and honour come from you; you are the ruler of all things. In your hands are strength and power to exalt and give strength to all (1 Chronicles, 29:11-12)

God's sovereignty is manifested on earth through the person of Jesus Christ, who appoints St Peter and his successors as responsible for the governance of the Church.

When Jesus came to the region of Caesarea Philippi, he asked his disciples, 'Who do people say the Son of Man is?'

They replied, 'Some say John the Baptist; others say Elijah; and still others, Jeremiah or one of the prophets.'

> *'But what about you?' he asked. 'Who do you say I am?'*
>
> *Simon Peter answered, 'You are the messiah, the Son of the living God.'*
>
> *Jesus replied, 'Blessed are you, Simon son of Jonah, for this was not revealed to you by flesh and blood, but by my Father in heaven. And I tell you that you are Peter, and on this rock I will build my church and the gates of Hades will not overcome it. I will give you the keys of the kingdom of heaven; whatever you bind on earth will be bound in heaven, and whatever you loose on earth will be loosed in heaven'* (Matthew, 16:13-19).

The Christian Church had grown up within the Roman Empire as a separate self-contained world, sometimes tolerated and sometimes persecuted but always an alien presence, until its adoption as the Empire's religion by Constantine in 312. But this long incubation within Rome ensured the separation between the sacred and the secular, which had been given authority in Matthew, 22:21 where Jesus says:

> *'Render to Caesar the things that are Caesar's; and to God the things that are God's.*

In the hierarchy of the Roman Catholic West, with the Pope as the head of the Church, the Lords Spiritual had precedence over the Lords Temporal, and the cathedral over the castle. Sacred knowledge and the administering of the sacraments were entirely the province of the Lords Spiritual. The Church had its own governance, and its officiates were subject to Canon Law. The Lords Temporal were responsible for the governance and defence of the realm, and the people were subject to Common or Roman law. This split in authority between the sacred and secular made for a fragile balance, but one that nonetheless held together for a millennium, producing a God-centred world that was deeply imbued with the Christian virtues.

There were two distinct halves to this millennium, and the year 1000 was the watershed between them. The first half came closest to realising the Christian ideal, and began with the conversion of the newly-conquering Germanic tribes. Two great saints were instrumental in this process: St Benedict of Nursia (d. 547) and St Gregory the Great (d. 604). St Gregory consolidated the power of the Papacy, sent out missionaries to all parts of the continent, including the far-away island of Britain, and was responsible for unifying Europe under the Catholic Church. St Benedict is recognized as the founder of Western Christian monasticism and his *Rule of St Benedict* profoundly influenced all subsequent monastic orders. He is known as a patron saint of Europe.

St Benedict's importance lies in the fact that it was monks and nuns who were primarily responsible for Europe becoming a Christian world. They vowed to live lives governed by the monastic rules of poverty, chastity and obedience, and to sincerely follow in the footsteps of Jesus Christ. The world they encountered was one of tribes and villages, and the monastery became its heart, teaching and counselling, taking care of the poor, administering to the sick and bringing the community together in worship. Christianity flourished in this environment, as witnessed by the number of saints that belong to this period. One only has to read the *Ecclesiastical History of the English People* composed in the 8th century by the Venerable Bede to get an idea of the light that shone through and illuminated their world.

This world was changing, however; towns were forming around the monasteries and trade was quickening; kings were consolidating their lands and their power. The papacy split with Byzantium over doctrine in 1054 and launched the First Crusade against Islam in 1095. Western Christendom was growing in power and confidence. The encounter with the Islamic world was critical to Western Christendom's cultural and intellectual evolution. The Crusades were taking place in Spain and the Holy Land. As soon as cities were conquered by the Crusaders, captive engineers and craftsmen were sent back into Christendom and their skills contributed to a building programme of incredible scale within the Church. Hundreds of magnificent cathedrals and abbeys and tens of thousands of fine parish churches in the new Gothic tradition appeared across Europe. Their size, which dwarfed all that was around them, manifested the absolute dominance of the sacred over the secular.

However, the Church was increasingly becoming a temporal power with its vast land holdings and fabulous wealth in treasure. Many cardinals and bishops were hardly distinguishable from their temporal lords. Cracks began to form between the power of the Church and the monarchs. The murder of St Thomas a Becket in 1170 was an early sign in England. King Henry II attempted to bring the Church under the jurisdiction of the Crown. St Thomas resisted and his martyrdom turned him into one of the greatest saints of Western Christendom. This event contributed to ensuring that the Church would remain the supreme authority for another three hundred years.

Finally, however, the authority of the Church was usurped by the power of kings. In England, Henry VIII became head of the Church and took his revenge on St Thomas a Becket; his remains were exhumed and burnt, and a royal proclamation announced that, henceforth, he was to be regarded as a traitor rather than a saint. Once Henry VIII had assumed control of the Church, he dissolved and destroyed nearly a thousand great abbeys, priories, convents and friaries. A third of the wealth of England was taken into the Royal coffers. The shrines of the saints in abbeys, cathedrals and churches were dismantled and their bones scattered. Entire social networks of education, labour and support for the poor and sick were destroyed along with the buildings. There had never been a destruction committed by a society on itself to compare with it. The thousand-year contemplative heart of Christianity in England was ripped out.

The beneficiary of the transfer of the vast accumulated wealth of the monasteries was the newly ennobled, rising merchant class, who would acquire their lands. In Christendom, merchants were somewhat despised and occupied a lowly place in the Vocational Triad, but now, banding together and forming companies, they were ready to take full advantage of this fast-developing new age. Meanwhile the kings, overstepping their rightful place, drew more and more power to themselves until absolute monarchies emerged. Charles V in Spain, Charles I in England, Louis XIV in France, and Peter the Great in Russia all rose to claim this status. The power of these new sovereign rulers and the triumph of the secular over the sacred rested on a new political entity that emerged out of the conflict that engulfed Christendom during the Reformation, namely the sovereign state.

The most intense warfare between Catholic and Protestant took place in the Germanic lands which were divided into many principalities and bishoprics, and at the Peace of Westphalia (1648), which ended the Thirty Years War, a formulation was put together that allowed each state to choose which form of Christianity it would adopt, and for their decision to be accepted by the other states. Judicial recognition was now given to a new kind of state that had been developing for more than a hundred years: the sovereign nation state. This ushered in a fundamental change in the identity of the individual. For a thousand years the primary unifying identity of the individual was Christian; after that came the relationship and obligations between subjects and their rulers, the local attachment to place, and other factors. With the collapse of Christendom, the primary unifying identity was subsumed into the newly-formed sovereign nation state. What had been a Christian identity became a kind of quasi-sacred national identity.

An artificial structure was being created in the wake of the collapse of Christendom. In this new framework, single cultures sharing a common language, religion and history, with stable geographical borders, fared best. As the power at the centre increased and communication systems developed, a process of homogenization took place, and the diversity within regions began to fade away. Portugal, Spain, France, England and the Netherlands were the first sovereign states to appear and between them would conquer and transform the world. But the world they conquered was multi-ethnic, multi-lingual, multi-cultural, multi-religious and highly complex. The imposition of the European model of the nation state would become a recipe for unstable and irrational political entities and continuous conflict and oppression.

The tyranny of the absolute monarchs finally led to rebellion and revolution, and either the elimination of monarchy or its reduction to an ever-weakening symbolic role. Sovereignty was now transferred to, and vested in the people, with democracy becoming the new ideal. In the euphoria of revolution, the philosophers and thinkers of what came to be known as the Enlightenment, envisioned a world where humanity would live in a state of equality, brotherhood and freedom.

But it was Luther who paved the way for what was to become the defining characteristic of Western civilisation with the vesting of sovereignty in the individual. This is explained in Richard Rex's book, *The Making of Martin Luther*:

> [Luther's] central doctrine, 'justification by faith alone', was meant to give each individual believer absolute certainty of enjoying the grace and favour of God... The underlying individualism of what would later be termed 'the personal relationship with God' passed into the DNA of liberal Protestantism and from there into most facets of Western culture.

Immanuel Kant then cemented the idea of individual autonomy in his definition of the Enlightenment.

> Enlightenment is man's emergence from his self-incurred immaturity. Immaturity is the inability to use one's own understanding without the guidance of another. The motto of enlightenment is therefore: *Sapere aude*! Have courage to use your own understanding.

This abandonment of authority was a reaction to the abuse of power by despotic kings and the endless religious disputes engulfing Christianity. Kant's investing the individual with an essentially subjectivist rational sovereignty would have far-reaching consequences further down the line. Being himself a Pietist Lutheran, he could not imagine what would happen when faith was taken out of the equation and religion, with its moral prohibitions, parked in a siding. A hundred years later Friedrich Nietzsche could see it:

> God is dead. God remains dead. And we have killed him. Yet his shadow still looms. How shall we comfort ourselves, the murderers of all murderers? What was holiest and mightiest of all that the world has yet owned has bled to death under our knives; who will wipe this blood off us? What water is there for us to clean ourselves?

Nietzsche prophesied that in the 20th century humanity would experience wars of unimaginable horror, and in the 21st century the machines of his invention would turn on him and the crisis of nihilism would come to a head. His crazed solution was for man to transcend himself and replace God by becoming Superman. Ironically, the consequences of this idea gave credence to the megalomaniacs who, in the 20th century, plunged the world into the horrors he had prophesied.

Over the last five hundred years, the West has gone on a journey that began with absolute sovereignty being vested in God, then with it passing into the monarchy and the sovereign nation state, then being vested in the people through democracy, and finally ending up with the sovereignty of the individual.

2

CIVILISATION

ISLAM

FOR A THOUSAND YEARS, before the rise of the European empires, the two civilisations that dominated the Afro-Eurasian world were those of China and Islam. They both represented powerful examples of the criterion of balance but were very different manifestations. China was an ancient world with a continuous history stretching back millennia, where balance depended on the establishment of the just empire with the Emperor as the mediator between Heaven and Earth. The cycles of the rise and fall of empires followed a course of order, disintegration and then order once again. But each time, fundamental characteristics remained the same; the presence of the Emperor, the Chinese language and script, the continuous wisdom of Confucius and the concept of Yin and Yang ensured that in each iteration balance was re-established and maintained through the force of dynamic equilibrium. This force guaranteed the unchanging, permanent character of the civilisation, which would be misread by the Enlightenment as stagnation. Each new dynasty had a particular character and would emphasize certain traits, but the core remained constant.

Whilst China was bound by its geography, what is known as Dār al-Islām (the Abode of Islam) had taken root from West Africa to China, binding together a myriad of different races, language groups and cultures into one civilisation. In the early 14th century a scholar from Tangiers, Ibn Battūta, spent 27 years travelling to every part of the world of Islam. Not only could he practise his profession as a *qādī* (judge) in India and the Maldives, he could converse with scholars in Timbuktu, Konya, Tabriz, Delhi, Malacca and Hangzhou. The Islamic system of governance, education and the sharia supported a civilisation unlike any that had appeared before.

But let us begin with the birthplace of this new civilisation. In the early part of the 7th century, the Arabian Peninsula was strategically placed to connect into the civilised worlds of Afro-Eurasia. By land, it buffered the warring empires of Byzantium and Persia, whilst it was linked by sea both to India, which was divided into many states, and to China, which was being unified under the Tang Dynasty. To the north, the Eurasian Steppes were dominated by the Turkish nomads whose empire had stretched from Manchuria to the borders of Hungary, but was now breaking up. To the North West, Christian monks were converting the Germanic tribes that had conquered the Western Roman Empire, and far to the East, Buddhism was entering Japan. The emergence of Islam out of the deserts of Arabia would, over the following centuries, utterly transform this world.

Mecca, the birth place of the Prophet, was a trading station on the route that connected the Indian Ocean and the Mediterranean Sea, and was the sacred centre for the Arab tribes who would come together in their annual pilgrimage to the Holy Kaaba. In this closely-knit society of warriors and traders, the Qur'an was transmitted through the person whom Muslims believe to be the last of the prophets and the 'Seal of Prophethood'. For thirteen years, Muhammad and his companions were in Mecca, enduring extreme hardship and persecution. In this hostile environment, the nascent community was sustained and encouraged by suras that were revealed during this time, and by the example and guidance of the Prophet; thus they were taught patience and trust in God, and compassion for their persecutors. In this period of trial, the Muslim inner life of submission and serenity was formed.

With the Hijra, the migration to Medina in the year 622, the Islamic calendar and era began. For ten years the Prophet led, governed and guided his community in the light of the revelations that continued to be transmitted, providing the framework of how to live as a society in a state of submission to the will of God. After these twenty-three years had passed, the Qur'an was complete and the Prophet departed this world, leaving a community immersed in the religion and ready to carry Islam onto the world stage.

Fundamental to the structure of Islamic society, as it would grow into its civilisational form, was the vocational triad that was manifested in the person of the Prophet. Firstly, he represented the scholar as the transmitter of revelation and the fount of wisdom; secondly, he was the ruler of his community and a warrior who led them in battle, and finally, he lived in a community of merchants and engaged in trade. Moreover, the Prophet is also regarded as having realised the perfect balance between inward and outward, between the life of the contemplative and the active life of family and society. All the various types of humanity could identify with the Prophet and seek to follow his exemplary conduct or *sunna*, which was preserved and transmitted through the Hadith, the corpus of sayings passed down from him. The all-encompassing character of the Prophet dissolved the rigidity of caste and vocation, allowing for a fluidity to exist, so that sultans might practise crafts, merchants become learned, and scholars engage in trade.

What came to be known as the Five Pillars of Islam formed the foundation for the religious life of all Muslims for all time. First amongst them is the attestation of faith (*shahāda*), that is, bearing witness to the Unity of God, and the prophethood of Muhammad. Then come the canonical prayers (*salāt*), to be performed five times each day. This is followed by the *zakāt* which is the annual tax paid by every wealthy Muslim and used to assure an equitable society. Fourthly, we have the month-long fast of Ramadan, a festival that combines ascetical self-denial, the celebration of giving, the communal partaking in the breaking of the fast, and a sacred commemoration of the revelation of the Qur'an, which began during the month of Ramadan. Finally, there is the Hajj or pilgrimage to Mecca, incumbent upon a believer if he or she is able, which brings together Muslims from across the globe in a visible testimony to unity.

These Five Pillars provide the framework for the Islamic way of life; they are common to all Muslims, and have never changed. Accepted by mainstream Sunnis and Shia alike, they provide a simple unifying structure that guides believers through the cycles of the day and year, and can be practised in any environment and terrain. The testimony of faith grounds all human experience in an affirmation of the oneness of God and of the prophethood of Muhammad. The five prayers ensure that all of human life, at home, in the market, even on a journey or in battle, is permeated by a living connection to, and dialogue with, God. *Zakāt* blesses the wealth of the rich, and provides succour to the poorest in society. The fast of Ramadan unifies the community during the sacred month, encouraging all believers to practise self-restraint and experience privation. The Hajj brings together believers from all corners of the Islamic world. It is a great leveller, with everyone leaving behind their wealth and status and donning simple white clothing, and it is a reminder of the gathering that is promised at the Resurrection.

The Qur'an, the Hadith of the Prophet and the Five Pillars of Islam would provide the unchanging kernel out of which the civilisation would evolve. When this stable, permanent sacred core engaged with the great civilisations of Afro-Eurasia, a dynamic process of transformation took place as the knowledge required in order to move from the tribal world of Arabia to a fully developed civilisation was assessed and assimilated. The rapid conquest, which produced an empire stretching from the Atlantic in the west to the borders of China and India in the east, called for the knowledge of statecraft and complex administration. This was acquired from Byzantium and Persia, ensuring a smooth transition of authority. The unity of Islamic civilisation was guaranteed by its sacred core, and its diversity by the way in which Islam was able to sift and embrace the different cultural forms and knowledge systems that were encountered.

Over a period of some five hundred years, the various aspects of the civilisation emerged and were refined, until at every level it was fully formed. The intellectual sciences were unified, the hierarchy of knowledge was established, the sharia reached its maturity, colleges and educational institutions were founded, craft and merchant guilds set up, and *tarīqas* (spiritual orders) to regulate the Sufi path came into being. Islamic civilisation had now reached a state of *mīzān*, that enabled each and every Muslim to live their lives in a spiritual, intellectual, moral and material environment that reflected the divine unity.

We have become used to believing the famous saying 'change is the only constant in life', and the idea that what doesn't change is stagnant and dying. However, when viewed from the perspective of *mīzān*, maintained through dynamic equilibrium, the opposite is true. At this point, it may be useful to use the analogy of the game of chess. The rules governing chess, once established, have remained the same for hundreds of years. It is difficult to imagine how they could be improved. The form is perfect. There have been millions of players of the game who have derived great pleasure from playing, but very few grand masters. However, the grand masters can never exhaust the possibilities that the game affords.

The sharia formed the backbone of Islamic civilisation and is a term that has been thoroughly misunderstood in the West. It is usually referred to as Islamic Law and tends to be viewed simply as a penal code. But this is only one aspect of a vast all-encompassing spiritual, moral and ethical system of how to live on this earth as a Muslim. It defines the relationships and obligations that obtain between the Muslim and his Creator, his fellow human beings and the creation. It is a comprehensive framework for the maintenance of *mīzān.* It was produced by scholars, and came into being through the process of instructing, guiding and counselling the community. Only when it was breached were legal sanctions applied.

The sharia was faithfully maintained by the scholars and was universally applied throughout the world of Islam. It took time to be formed, but after some five hundred years scholars could survey a system that had grown organically, and were able to draw out universal principles that facilitated the flowering of the developed sciences of the Maxims of Sacred Law (*qawāʿid al-fiqh*) and the Principles of Sacred Law *(usūl al-fiqh)* and with it, the maturity of the system.

As they formulated the sharia, the scholars drew upon the Revelation, as well as the sayings and conduct of the Prophet, in order to legislate for everything from ablution, prayer, charity and pilgrimage, to trade, property rights, agricultural ethics, marriage and inheritance, as well as every other aspect of human life, whether personal or social. Their issuing of legal edicts to address particular, sometimes wholly new problems, was another of the scholar's important roles. From advising the faithful on their marital obligations, to admonishing a ruler to desist from a war not authorised by sharia, the scholar as politically-neutral interpreter of revelation held a position of immunity that the ruler only violated at his peril.

At the heart of Islamic civilisation is the term *adab*, which is sometimes translated as 'manners' or 'etiquette'. These words, however, suggest a kind of surface polishing to a person's conduct, something artificial even, which is far from the true meaning of *adab*. RA Nicholson, the celebrated translator of Arabic and Persian literature, rendered the term *adab* in English as 'spiritual culture', and this expression does capture something of the essential nature of *adab*, which is a deeply-rooted spirituality and sense of the sacred that infuses a person's inner demeanour as well as their outer conduct. To have *adab* is to have an inbuilt sense of propriety such that one gives each person, each act and each thing its due. There is said to be an *adab* towards God, an *adab* towards one's fellow human beings and an *adab* towards one's self. The word derives from the Arabic root which has the meaning of educating, training and discipline, as indicated in a saying of the Prophet, from whose example all *adab* is said to derive, *'My Lord educated me and made my education (adab) beautiful'.*

The three ways of life, urban, rural and nomadic, also reached a state of *mīzān* within the world of Islam. The interplay between city and nomad is brilliantly observed in Ibn Khaldun's 15th century work, *The Muqadimmah – an Introduction to History.* Ibn Khaldūn explains how the nomadic way of life fostered the martial spirit and self-reliance. The nomads come out of the desert, conquer the cities and sultanates and establish their ruling dynasties. In time, the life of the city corrupts and softens the rulers who are in their turn conquered by other nomads who set up their dynasties and the cycle is repeated. The two great areas of nomadism, the southern deserts inhabited by the Arabs, and the northern Steppes of Eurasia, inhabited by the Turks and Mongols, provided most of the ruling dynasties of the central lands of Dār al-Islām.

The simplicity and austerity of the nomadic way of life connected deep into the fabric of Islamic civilisation. The carpets on which they sat and the tents that sheltered them were all made from the wool and hair of their flocks of sheep and goats, and herds of camels. The carpet, in palace, home and mosque, became a defining feature of the civilisation.

The nomads played a key role in trade, providing the transportation, cameleers and guides. As well as rearing animals which produced meat for the cities, they were breeders of horses and camels for the armies of the dynasties, and provided an endless supply of recruits for the military.

Most people lived on the land and grew the food and materials they needed to support themselves, whilst the surplus was traded in the cities or delivered as tax to the authorities. A symbiosis existed in many areas between the farmers and nomads that greatly benefitted the land; nomads would run their animals over the lands of the farmers, feeding on the stubble and fertilising the soil, after which the farmers would plant their crops.

The city was the centre of Islamic civilisation, with its markets, craft workshops, educational institutions, spiritual centres, law courts and governor's palace. From the cities, through trade and the example of the pious merchant, Islam reached the furthest points of Afro-Eurasia, and through the spread of the Sufi orders, deep into the countryside. What is clear is that Islam spread remarkably easily and once established, was loved and cherished by city dwellers, nomads and villagers alike.

Islam succeeded in creating a stable, sustainable, universal civilisation which maintained the *mīzān* through the process of dynamic equilibrium. Generations of

Muslims cherished their Holy Book, loved their Prophet, were happy in their religion, were at home in their culture and found peace in their civilisation.

THE WEST

JESUS CHRIST WAS BORN in a province of the Roman Empire at a time when it was reaching its height. For three hundred years, Christianity was an underground movement, sometimes tolerated and at other times persecuted. The Christian Church became a self-contained spiritual society within the civilisation of Rome. The Roman Empire was divided between the Greek-speaking East and the Latin-speaking West. When the emperor Constantine converted to Christianity in 312, he moved the centre of gravity to the East and founded the new capital of Constantinople, which became known as the second Rome. By the beginning of the 5th century, the Western Roman Empire had collapsed and was divided up between a number of Germanic tribes.

In the East, in what became known as Byzantium, Christianity transformed a living Roman Empire with all its civilised administration and framework in place. In the West, Christianity had to contend with a tribal village world to which it brought a belief system and way of life. With the Crusades, beginning with the conquest of Jerusalem in 1099, Western Christendom began to engage with the worlds of both Islam and Byzantium. Urbanisation increased with markets rapidly developing and cities forming. However, the monastic Christianity of the West did not have the framework for the transition from a mainly rural society to a fully developed urban civilisation. So there took place the strangest of events: the Renaissance. A civilisation that had been dead and buried for a thousand years, was disinterred and co-opted to fulfil this role.

The Greco-Roman 'Classical World', as it was now called, was believed to have reached the summit of civilisation and became the ideal that had to be emulated. Religion and culture became separated: the warrior replaced the saint at the apex of society; the Greek and Latin classics replaced the Bible at the centre of education; museums were built to house the remains of the Classical World so that they could be preserved and studied; classical architecture replaced the vernacular forms that had grown up naturally within Christendom, creating an orderly, but contrived environment; the artist brought the Gods down from heaven into the human dimension, and the glorification of God and the saints was replaced by the glorification of Man. Man now became 'the measure of all things'.

But it was a new detached being that looked out upon the world. No longer belonging to an organic culture, this being was mesmerised by a dead world, which through the imagination had been brought back to life and idealised. Culture was no longer formed from inside, it would now be acquired from outside, from a source that was dead. We pass from an age when the Christian was formed through an integrated process, to one in which civilisation was acquired through learning about another world that existed in another time. This produced a new kind of 'civilised' being who, living in an idealised imaginary world, was more at home with dead cultures and civilisations than with those that were alive.

The social impact of the Renaissance was to separate the elite from the rest of society. Classical education and culture had no meaning for the mass of society, which had no access to it. However, it provided the framework for the creation of a warrior caste. The martial virtues of courage, self-sacrifice and discipline were elevated and celebrated, eclipsing the Christian virtues of love, forgiveness and humility. In literature, the lives of the saints were replaced by the exploits of the heroes. Statues of the great warriors and statesmen were erected in the squares and public spaces, and their 'Roman' palaces dominated city and countryside. Finally, in death, the Church honoured them, housing their tombs and memorials in churches and cathedrals.

The Roman Empire became the model and inspiration for the newly-formed sovereign states to create their own empires. Unable to conquer their neighbours, they went overseas and imposed upon the world their version of civilisation, destroying the living worlds they encountered and placing the remains of their artefacts in the newly-created museums where they could be studied.

Meanwhile, the Renaissance wreaked havoc within the Christian Church and penetrated deep into the Papacy. For a hundred years, from the middle of the 15th to the middle of the 16th century, a series of popes, steeped in the new humanism, behaved like the most decadent of Roman emperors to the disgust of the pious. They set about recreating the grandeur of Rome and rebuilding St Peter's in the classical style. To fund this grandiose scheme, the popes issued indulgences; the faithful could pay for their loved ones and themselves to have their time in Purgatory reduced. This was the fuse that set off the explosion that led to the Reformation and the ripping apart of Christendom.

The next great change came about at the end of the 18th century, when revolutions rocked America and France, resulting in humanism changing from being the study and emulation of the classical world into a subjective definition of the rights of each and every human being. These revolutions were the result of the exploitation of colonies, the injustice of absolute monarchs, the excesses and venality of their courts, the gulf that had grown between the ruling classes and the people, and the hypocrisy and intolerance of the churches. The successful revolutionaries wished to sweep away the old order and its hierarchies and create a new world which would benefit all people. A utopian future was envisaged in which heaven would be brought down to earth. Surveying the past in his book *Rights of Man*, Thomas Paine saw three clear stages unfolding:

> First, Superstition. Secondly, Power. Thirdly, the common interest of society, and the common rights of man. The first was a government of priest craft, the second of conquerors, and the third of reason.

A new narrative was forming in which the Christian Millennium was reduced to an age of darkness and superstition, followed by the tyranny of the kings. The revolutionaries, guided by pure reason, would now create the just society. The American Declaration of Independence famously captures this aspiration:

> We hold these truths to be self-evident, that all men are created equal, that they are endowed by their Creator with certain unalienable Rights, that among these are Life, Liberty and the pursuit of Happiness.

The French Revolution echoed this with its anthem of 'Liberty, Equality, Fraternity,' and the rights of humanity took centre stage. However, once the Creator was removed from the equation, what had been relative terms, employed in the response to tyranny, were transformed into absolutes. Fraternity became the foundational principle for the socialist doctrines that emerged out of the horrors of the Industrial Revolution, and freedom and equality became the twin pillars of humanism in what came to be known as the 'modern world'.

However, the secular understanding of freedom and equality took on an altogether different meaning in humanism than it had within Christianity. In Christianity, as in Islam, freedom is achieved when the carnal self is conquered. For the Christian, it is only through Christ that this is made possible, and it is only the saints who are truly free.

> *But now you are free from the power of sin. You have become a servant for God. Your life is set apart for God-like living. The end is life that lasts forever.* (Romans, 6:22)

Likewise, it is only under God and in Christ that we are equal.

> *There is neither Jew nor Greek, there is neither slave nor free, there is no male or female, for you are all one in Christ.* (Galatians, 3:28).

Human rights came to the fore again after World War II when, responding to the barbarity of what had taken place, the Universal Declaration of Human Rights was enshrined in the United Nations Charter. This then became the model for legislation to be enacted in the European Union and many nation states.

Whilst the post-colonial nations were grappling with real problems of tyranny, exploitation and fundamental human freedoms, the affluent post-war West was taking freedom and equality into an altogether different sphere with the enshrinement of the sovereignty of the self, the Sexual Revolution of the 1960's, and the moral relativism of post-modernism. The pursuit of happiness, freed from its Christian moorings, would produce a sybaritic society with the freedom to indulge itself in whatever ways that could be manufactured and marketed by the new corporations.

To summarise, Western Christendom's inability to make the transition from a rural to an urban civilisation ushered in the Renaissance, and the idealisation of a dead world. With 'Man becoming the measure of all things' humanism was born. In that which now regarded itself as the civilised world, humanism aspired to the virtues of the classical age. With the descent into our modern world, humanism has been transformed into the rights demanded by, and granted to, the sovereign individual.

3
KNOWLEDGE

ISLAM

WITHIN A HUNDRED YEARS of the establishment of the community in Medina, the Muslims had control of an empire that stretched from Spain to India and the borders of China, and contained within it the richest provinces of the Byzantine Empire and the entire Persian Empire. As it encountered a world of many ancient cultures and civilisations in various stages of decay, a remarkable process of synthesis took place. The West mistook these early centuries, when the knowledge of the world was being sifted and sorted, for the 'Golden Age of Islam'. It was, in fact, the formative stage, and what was remarkable was the universal civilisation that would later emerge.

At this point, it is important to understand the difference between the Islamic and modern understanding of what constitutes verifiable knowledge. For the modern mindset that traces its origins to the revolutions of the 16th and 17th centuries, verifiable knowledge has been reduced to what can be discovered through the scientific method and is limited to the material realm. Everything else belongs to the imagination and is entirely subjective. In Islam, verifiable knowledge is understood to exist in all three realms of the unseen, human and material, and can be attained through the Revelation and correct reasoning. This is where Islam differed fundamentally from Christianity. In Christianity, certain doctrines have come to require the setting aside of reason, whereas in Islam, it is an obligation that the Revelation be affirmed through reason.

The Qur'an and the life of the Prophet are the foundations on which Islamic civilisation was built. During his life, every action of the Prophet was recorded by his companions, and a science was developed to ensure that the proper transmission of this knowledge from generation to generation took place. Muslim scholars expended much effort in preserving, transmitting and interpreting the Revelation. The twenty-three years of prophecy and revelation are traditionally known as *ʿasr al-saʿāda*, which can be translated as the 'age of bliss'. When this blessed period came to an end and the scholars, both men and women, were left to fend for themselves, an immense intellectual ferment took place.

This was the time when the mereological principle that 'the whole can contain the part, but the part cannot contain the whole' was tested. Among the restrictive positions taken during this formative period were those of the *Muʿtazilites*, who claimed for reason the ultimate authority, the *Hashwiyya*, who insisted on the literal interpretation of the text, and the *Bātinists* who sought only to understand the inner or symbolic meaning of the Qur'an. However, the parts claiming the whole were gradually drawn into the upward trajectory, and the mereological principle realised. In time, philosophers and theologians were to discover the synthesis in which the four fundamental sources of knowledge: revelation (*naql*), mystical cognition (*dhawq*), reason (*ʿaql*) and sensation (*ihsās*), were brought into a state of *mīzān*, and the unity at the heart of Islam was unveiled.

This journey of discovery involved the contribution of many great thinkers. Foremost among these were: Ibn Sīnā (Avicenna, d. 1037), who transformed philosophy and developed a universal science of metaphysics that could encompass all of the sciences and simultaneously attain the heights necessary for an adequate intellectual treatment of the Revelation; Imam al-Ghazālī (d. 1111), whose monumental work recognized the mystic path as reaching the highest knowledge of God attainable within a framework that acknowledged the value and relationality of every field of human knowledge; Fakhr al-Dīn al-Rāzī (d. 1209), who by applying his epoch-making intellectual power to a synthesis of Avicennan general metaphysics and the revelatory principles of speculative theology (*kalām*), created a new all-encompassing theology in which every branch of knowledge was shown to be part of a single truth, and paved the way for the great *summas* of the 14th and 15th centuries; and Ibn ʿArabī (d. 1240), known forever as 'the Greatest Master', who for the first time fully encompassed philosophy within his mystical vision and thus contracted a sublime marriage between them. By the 15th century, a synthesis of Akbārian, Avicennan and Rāzian thought was complete – powerfully exemplified in the works of later thinkers like Mulla Fenari (d. 1431) and Taşköprüzade (d. 1560) in the Ottoman world – and a hierarchy of knowledge had been established that took in the revealed sciences alongside all of the branches of philosophy and mysticism. This hierarchy would come to be adopted in the higher educational systems of both the Ottoman Empire and the Mughal Empire in India.

In this hierarchy of knowledge, those sciences pertaining to the knowledge of God, the spiritual and the metaphysical, were the highest, and those relating to the corporeal, the limited and the material, the lowest. Everything had its place, and when it was in its rightful position, *mīzān* was achieved. When looking at Islam, the Enlightenment in Europe saw only its achievement in the material sciences, which was indeed considerable. The Muslims received everything they could from the civilisations they were encountering that supported and conformed to the Islamic way of life: the zero, which made possible advances in the mathematical sciences, came from India; medicine and geometry from the Greeks; astronomy from the Greeks and Persians; statecraft from the Persians and papermaking from the Chinese. All were integrated, and some were further developed to enable Islamic civilisation to function. However, in Islam the material sciences did not take off on their own as they did in the West; rather, they formed part of a whole that, once established, was maintained and renewed by each generation. As an example, the astrolabe came from the Greeks, was improved by the Muslims, and then remained unchanged for a thousand years performing the same task perfectly. Engagement with the physical world was kept within bounds and was there to support a holistic way of life.

From the earliest period, there evolved within Islam the spiritual and ethical science which came to be known as Sufism (*tasawwuf*, later also known in Shiʿism as *ʿirfān*). Sufism embodied a subtle understanding of the inner make-up of the human being and a system of practices that focused on disciplining and purifying the soul or self (*nafs*), that could bring the believer to attain sincerity of worship, and a state in which he or she might be granted experiential cognition or mystical knowledge of God (*maʿrifa*). This spiritual science embraced and developed another triad which has its origin in the Qur'an, and which defines three stages or stations in the journey of the soul: the evil-inciting soul (*al-nafs al-ammāra bi'l-sūʾ*, Qur'an, 12:53), the self-reproaching soul (*al-nafs al-lawwāma*, Qur'an, 75:2) and the soul at peace (*al-nafs al-mutma'inna*, Qur'an, 89:27). The hierarchy in the realm of knowledge and the higher educational system that grew up embodying it, ensured that the spiritual sciences were properly protected.

The protection of Sufism and its place within the mainstream knowledge system ensured that it was accessible to any person who wished to follow the path to purify themselves and attain inner peace. In Christendom it was in the monastery that this peace was sought by the monks and nuns; in Islam it was available to all, from courtiers to scholars, merchants, craftsmen and husbandmen, both men and women.

The traditional Islamic city has been described as a family monastery, engaging the whole community in a spiritual way of life – a way of life that permeated the whole civilisation.

In Islam, all of the sciences existed within a framework of unity, harmony, and mutual interdependence, crowned by metaphysics and theology. The sciences were there exactly to produce a genuine 'theory of everything'. It allowed for the individual to know and experience the reality of existence through the soul's receptivity to revelation, the mystical cognition of the spirit, the reasoning of the mind and the acuity of the senses.

The system of knowledge and the sharia, with its different levels and disciplines, spread right across Dār al-Islām, and scholars could travel, live and work almost anywhere in this unified cultural world. The multifaceted nature of the scholar's engagement is beautifully described by Ross Dunn in his introduction to *The Adventures of Ibn Battuta*, when enumerating the different streams of travel and migration in which Ibn Battūta, the scholar, participated;

> First, he was a pilgrim, joining the march of pious believers to the spiritual shrines of Mecca and Medina at least four times in his career. Second, he was a devotee of Sufism, or mystical Islam, travelling, as thousands did, to the hermitages and lodges of venerable holy men to receive their

blessing and wisdom. Third, he was a juridical scholar, seeking knowledge and erudite company in the great cities of the Islamic heartland. And finally, he was a member of the literate, mobile, world-minded elite, an educated adventurer as it were, looking for hospitality, honours, and profitable employment in the more newly-established centres of Islamic civilization in the further regions of Asia and Africa. In any of these travelling roles, however, he regarded himself as a citizen, not of a country called Morocco, but of Dar al-Islam, to whose universalist spiritual, moral and social values he was loyal above any other allegiance.

THE WEST

AT THE DAWN OF THE 16th century, when the synthesis of knowledge was taking place in Islam, Western Christendom was in turmoil and being torn apart. As well as the cultural divide brought about by the Renaissance, there lay at the heart of this schism a profound theological problem within Christianity: the relationship between faith and reason. The problem did not arise until a higher understanding of logic, philosophy and metaphysics was introduced through the works of Avicenna (Ibn Sīnā) and Averroes (Ibn Rushd). Aquinas in his *Summa Theologiae* attempted to achieve the synthesis that had been realised in

Islam but was unable to do so. Reason encountered fundamental contradictions when approaching the Incarnation and the Trinity. The Catholics did their best to keep reason within the domain of the sacred by allowing faith in the Christian dogmas to coexist with reason, in a marriage of convenience that was somehow resolved in heaven.

However, Martin Luther did not mince his words regarding his attitude towards reason:

> Reason is a whore, the greatest enemy that faith has; it never comes to the aid of spiritual things, but more frequently than not struggles against the divine Word, treating with contempt all that emanates from God.

Thus, the Protestants, believing faith to be the only way of approaching the Deity, abandoned reason wholly to the secular realm with far-reaching consequences. The material realm became the only field with which reason could engage; it had no place in religion. The natural philosopher, embedded in the material world, arose, and in time would mutate into the modern scientist, who would eventually lay claim to all verifiable knowledge concerning our existence.

The recently-emerged detached perspective of the Renaissance scholar, and the banishment of reason to the material realm, produced a new relationship with the natural world, which is chillingly described by Francis Bacon in his *Novum Organum*. Nature would now be rendered the 'slave of mankind', and her secrets extracted by placing her 'under constraint and vexed; that is to say, when by art and the hand of man, she is forced out of her natural state, and squeezed and moulded.' The new sciences do not 'merely exert a gentle guidance over nature's course; they have the power to conquer and subdue her, to shake her to her foundations.' This desire to conquer, control and exploit nature was to erupt in a Protestant land, and that land would be England. The separation of faith and reason that had taken place within Protestantism ensured that the rational mind would be wholly focused on a material world that had been stripped of its spiritual meaning. But it was a French Catholic, Descartes, now thinking within the constraints of natural philosophy, who introduced the mechanistic way of looking at the world: 'I have described this earth, and indeed this whole visible world, as a machine'. Within a century, Isaac Newton was to set in motion the image of the Clockwork Universe. Humanity was now on the way to manifesting this philosophy in the creation of a machine culture.

What took place was a breaching of the mereological principle: 'the whole can contain the part, but the part cannot contain the whole.' Reason's attempt to claim all knowledge reduced the human being to a thinking machine. The separation and descent of reason, accompanied by the senses, to the corporeal realm, set in motion the aberrations and myopia of a world created by the rational mind that was divorced from its natural context, and incapable of knowing or experiencing the whole. And we are surrounded by the effects of the unintended consequences that have inevitably ensued. In what follows I have outlined some of the most damaging.

Thomas Newcomen was an ironmonger by trade and a Baptist lay preacher by calling. In the 1720s, he invented the first coal-fired steam engine to solve the problem of removing water from deep mines. He had no idea that the consequences of releasing the fossil fuels from under the earth and seas would be global warming and the possible destruction of life on earth.

Albert Einstein solved an equation that had been eluding mathematicians for decades and was celebrated for it. He had no idea that this was one of the critical steps that would lead to the creation of the atom bomb. 'If only I had known, I should have become a watchmaker,' he cried, and spent the rest of his life campaigning for nuclear disarmament.

DDT was hailed as a miracle product in the 1940s and 50s and its inventor, Paul Hermann Mueller, received the Nobel prize in 1949. In 1962, Rachel Carson's book exposed the devastating impact that DDT was having on wildlife.

Thomas Midgley was a celebrated mechanical engineer working for General Motors in the 1920s and 30s. He was responsible for two innovations. Firstly, to solve the knocking in car engines he added lead to petrol; for eighty years, all over the world, lead was spewed out into the environment, the toxic effects of which are still with us. His second invention was CFCs as a coolant in fridges and air conditioning; the consequence of this was to create a hole in the ozone layer. The environmental historian, JR McNeill stated: 'Midgley had more impact on the atmosphere than any single organism in the earth's history.'

The Belgian-American chemist, Leo Baekeland, was surprised by his invention. 'Well, it was kind of an accident, because plastic is not what I meant to invent.' Some accident! Plastics have contaminated the oceans, the rivers, the water we drink and the air we breathe. It is only now that we are beginning to understand the impact that plastics are having on our health and that of the planet.

Norman Borlaug was the mastermind behind the so-called Green Revolution that has been more aptly named the Chemical Revolution by the Indian conservationist and scientist Vandana Shiva. To produce super yields, the land has been poisoned, the water sucked out of the earth, and the traditional farming practices and knowledge destroyed. In India some 300,000 farmers have committed suicide in the last twenty-five years. In most of these cases it is because the imposition of chemical agriculture has plunged them into debt.

Alexander Fleming invented penicillin, a miracle addition to the armoury in the war against bugs. In the modern environment of factory farming, people crowding and global travel, the bugs fought back and mutated. Now we have a super problem. Dame Sally Davies, Chief Medical Officer for England, stated that if we don't reverse present trends, 'Superbugs will kill us before climate change.'

Research scientists at Cambridge University and other leading institutions around the world are engaged in two major activities. Either, like the British Antarctic Survey, they are dealing with the problems caused by the unintended consequences of the past, or they are going deeper and deeper into matter, like the Nanoscience Centre, no doubt producing the next generation of unintended consequences, which are likely to be even more serious. We are testing the Chthonic Principle to its limits: the deeper you go into matter, the more dangerous the forces that are released.

Nothing, however, demonstrates our perilous situation more than what is taking place in the science of Artificial Intelligence. Here we have the perfect scenario of man divorced from God playing God. In the 19th century, the idea that the scientist would create a living creature who would turn against his creator, was terrifying. The monster in Mary Shelley's novel, *Frankenstein*, embodied the nightmare. The early cinema took up the theme, and the mad scientist joined the repertoire as both a comedic and a terrifying figure.

However, scientists are now taking us into a far more dangerous and sinister world. They are creating a monster that makes Frankenstein's look pretty harmless. After all he could be dealt with. Two prominent scientists have been at the forefront of promoting the virtues of AI. Firstly, Professor Jim Al-Khalili, theoretical nuclear physicist, who in a recent BBC documentary, stated:

> AI is developing fast, no longer just relying on programmers telling it the rules, it's learning to do amazing things by itself, faster and sometimes even better than we can. What's more, it's started to discover ways of doing things we didn't know about. Now I don't believe there's any pixie dust that we have to sprinkle over the grey matter in our heads to bring about consciousness. There's nothing our brains do that couldn't in principle be replicated. I feel inspired by what AI can do today and I believe that, through AI, we'll greatly extend our own capacities, changing our lives in ways we can't yet imagine.

Second, is the American inventor and futurologist, Ray Kurzweil, who in an interview expressed the view that:

> [Chips] will go inside our brains, they'll connect our brains to the cloud, not just to do things like search and translate, but to actually extend the power of our thinking...and give us more neo-cortical modules and more hierarchy to our neo-cortex which will make us smarter, and enable us to create more profound music, to be funnier, to be more artistic, to basically enhance those qualities of humanity that we value.

This belief that, in time, the scientist will be able to entirely replicate the human brain and indeed enhance its operation, leads us into a further and chilling chapter of the narrative of progress. When I first saw the standard evolution picture, from ape to man, with the addition of a cyborg leading the charge, I thought it was supposed to be a joke. But the AI fanatics are deadly serious, they really believe the next stage in evolution is the cyborg.

It is difficult to know how to respond to such a total loss of understanding of the true nature of humanity and the miracle of Creation. The idea that a machine bound by algorithms can replicate the human being is absurd and profoundly disturbing. There are, in fact, many scientists who have expressed unease about the dangers that AI poses. Elon Musk went to the heart of the matter when he stated, 'With artificial intelligence we are summoning up the demon.' A worried Bill Gates surmised, 'I don't understand why some people are not concerned.' Stephen Hawking warned that 'Artificial intelligence could spell the end of the human race.'

Serious questions are also being asked about the extraordinary theories that science is positing regarding the universe. How certain is the idea that our universe is 95% made up of dark matter and dark energy? The Cambridge particle physicist, Dr Harry Cliff, in his lecture at the Royal Society, demonstrated the fragility of this theory:

> When you hear the word dark in physics, you should get very suspicious, because it basically means we don't know what we are talking about.

Other fantastical ideas are coming out of the scientific imagination. There is no empirical evidence for string theory, and in the case of multiverse theory, empirical evidence is not even possible.

In a documentary film made shortly before his death, Stephen Hawking was asked the question: 'In physics there are these two huge theories – Einstein's theory of relativity, and quantum mechanics. The Holy Grail for some time has been how can we draw these two together? It is what people refer to as the Theory of Everything. Do you think we will ever achieve that?' He answered: 'I think we will eventually discover a unified theory, though it may take longer than the twenty years I predicted forty-five years ago.'

There is a very simple reason why a 'theory of everything' eludes the scientists. The material realm of the scientist is part of a greater reality. The mereological principle stands; the part cannot contain the whole. The scientist's desire for unity is a fundamental and natural human aspiration, but it can only be realised through the totality of the human cognition.

The machine world we inhabit, which has come out of the imagination of the reasoning mind, could be described as a cult, if we define a cult as a world that only makes sense according to its own criteria and does not connect into reality. The Catholic historian Christopher Dawson observed that modern man was cut off from heaven and from the earth. Like spacemen, we exist in our own artificial creation. The modern cult is a death cult, forming its world out of the annihilation of all previous cultures and the destruction of the natural world. But for the modern cult to come to fruition there had to be a marriage between the scientist and the newly-liberated merchant, which I shall address in the following chapter.

4

COMMERCE

ISLAM

THE QUR'AN WAS revealed to a remote community that was astride one of the main arteries of trade and had control of a key product: incense. The role of merchant was embedded in the society, and numerous passages in the Qur'an are addressed to the merchant. Again, in these passages we see an emphasis on the need for balance and equity in buying and selling.

> *Those who, when they spend, are neither extravagant nor niggardly, but hold a just balance between those extremes.* (Qur'an, 25:67)

> *Fill the measure when you measure, and weigh with a right balance; that is better and fairer in the end.* (Qur'an, 17:35)

> *Woe to those who give short measure: those who, when they are to receive their due from people, demand that it be given in full – but when they have to measure or weigh that which they owe to others, give less than what is due!* (Qur'an, 83:1-3)

The early success of Islam opened up a vast world for merchant activity. Wealth poured into the community, and the scholars were faced with the danger of worldliness overcoming the *umma* or Islamic community. Many of the early works of scholarship address issues relating to commerce and how it should be practised in the light of Islam, and a significant portion of the sharia is devoted to defining and regulating the role of the merchant. Many hadith were cited:

> *May God's mercy be on he who is lenient in his buying, his selling and in recalling his debts.* (Bukhārī)

> *Give the labourer his wage, even before his sweat dries.* (Ibn Mājah)

> *Whoever grants one who has fallen upon hard times respite for a debt, or waives it for him, God will shelter him beneath His shade.* (Muslim)

In China and Christendom, the merchant inhabited a lowly and even despised position in society. However, in Islam the virtuous merchant was held in high regard.

> *The truthful, honest merchant shall be with the prophets, the righteous and the martyrs on the Day of Judgement.* (Tirmidhi)

The pious merchant became the cornerstone of Islamic civilisation. The markets were adjacent to the mosques, and whereas today, when walking through a Middle Eastern bazaar, pop music blares out of loud-speakers, in pre-modern times one would hear the murmuring of the Qur'an being recited. At the time of prayer, the market would go quiet, and if a famous scholar visited the city, traders would close their shops to attend his discourses.

Unlike the West where business is competitive, in Islam it was a collaborative endeavour. The markets were grouped according to their trades. The first sale of the day was believed to hold particular blessing. If, when a trader had already made a sale, another customer came to his stall and he noticed that a fellow trader was yet to make his first sale, he would direct the customer to his colleague's stall. If a trader fell on hard times, the other traders would club together to put him back on his feet. As the civilisation developed, these practices were formalised within guilds, which also encompassed the crafts.

The guilds were corporate bodies of merchants and craftsmen which regulated entry into trades, the equal treatment of guild members, the opening of shops, and the quality of work and products. The guilds also arbitrated disputes between members, and ensured prices were proportionate. As the novice was being trained in a trade or craft, he would be taught the moral and ethical codes of his profession. The guilds would often have a patron saint and initiation ceremonies, and thus imbued everyday work with an imprint of the sacred.

The importance in Islam of charity cannot be overstated and the distribution of surplus wealth by the merchant community contributed greatly to the creation of a caring and integrated society. The Qur'an is replete with exhortations regarding charity:

> *They ask you what they should spend. Say: 'Whatever you spend of good is for parents and kinsmen, orphans, the needy, and wayfarers. And all the good that you do, God knows it well.'* (Qur'an, 2:215)

There are also many hadiths relating to charity:

> *The Prophet Muhammad, blessings and peace be upon him, said: 'Charity is prescribed for each descendant of Adam every day the sun rises.' He was then asked: 'Of what should we give charity each day?' The Prophet answered: 'The doors of goodness are many: enjoining good, forbidding evil, removing harm from the road, listening to the deaf, leading the blind, guiding one to the object of his need, hurrying with the strength of one's legs to one in sorrow who is asking for help, and supporting the feeble with the strength of one's arms - all these are charity prescribed for you.'* (Bukhārī, Muslim)

> *When a person dies, his good works are cut off, all but three: ongoing charity, knowledge that others benefit from, and a righteous child who prays for him.* (Muslim)

Ongoing charity became institutionalised in the *waqf* or charitable endowment. The origin and acknowledged proof text for the *waqf*, alongside the last hadith cited above, is a narration which recounts how the Prophet directed ʿUmar ibn al-Khaṭṭāb to make some land he had acquired at Khaybar into a *waqf*, and made certain conditions pertaining to it, amongst which were that it was not to be sold, or inherited, or given as a gift; and that whoever was guardian over it could eat from it and feed a friend, but could not accumulate personal wealth from it. These principles formed the basis of an institution that would come to represent as much as half of the wealth of Islamic societies.

The merchants of Islam, deeply imbued with the knowledge and love of their religion, carried Islam as far as China in the East and present-day Nigeria in the West. Many of these merchants settled, becoming part of communities, and through their interactions with local people, settlements grew into cities and ancient cities were transformed as the civilisation took root. Dār al-Islām expanded through trade and was brought back to its centre through the pilgrimage to Mecca.

THE WEST

IN CHRISTENDOM, as we noted above, the merchant held a lowly place in the hierarchy. Most trade was local, with the Italian and Jewish merchants mainly responsible for long-distance trade, as they were connected into the Afro-Eurasian network. With the collapse of Christendom, the power of the merchant class rose. Jacob Fugger (d. 1525) was a German banker and business man who took full advantage of the changing times and is reputed to have become the richest man who has ever lived. He convinced Pope Leo X, who was from the Medici family of bankers, to lift the ban on usury. Charging interest was considered a sin in Christianity, Islam and Judaism. The Pope now indicated that interest was only usury if the loan was made 'without labour, cost or risk'. In his book, *The Richest Man Who Ever Lived*, the veteran journalist Greg Steinmetz states, 'Leo's decree was a breakthrough for capitalism. Debt financing accelerated. The modern economy was on its way.' The Dutch set up the first national bank and the other European nations followed. The merchants followed in the wake of the European conquerors, and the Dutch, English, French and other European nations set up trading companies, the proto corporations of today, covering all the territories they were engaged with. The stage was set for the act that would bring the merchant centre stage and usher in the Modern World. Natural philosophers had imagined the world as a machine, but it was the merchants and craftsmen who turned this idea into a reality.

Auguste Comte taught that the scientific method is the only guarantor of knowledge and that it had replaced metaphysics in man's social evolution. The study of human society and the human being moved across to the sciences, where the individual was examined and experimented upon, as though he or she were an animal composed of machine parts. The sovereignty of the individual, combined with his new animal status, prepared the human being to be the perfect subject for a world now ruled by the merchant.

But it took time for this commercial world to fully emerge. In Great Britain, throughout the 19th century, the new industries were simply replacing the old crafts. A revival of Christianity provided the moral teaching for society, and a classical education continued to civilise the Englishman. It was in the United States that the modern world was fully manifested. New business corporations emerged that took complete control over the material realm, providing everything that the human being needed, and then going on to produce whatever the human being could possibly desire. To comply with this new commercial society, the human being was renamed; whereas in Christendom people were Christians, and in our civilised world they aspired to be civilised human beings, in this brave new world they were redefined as consumers. The new corporations not only provided the traditional needs of housing, food and clothing, but moved into the areas of entertainment, recreation and education and became the conveyors of a new morality, with the influence of Church and a classical education dying away.

Whereas with the Renaissance, the classics and humanities had replaced the Bible and religion at the centre of the university curriculum, now the classics and humanities have been displaced by the sciences and business studies. The principal goal has now become innovation and entrepreneurship; you have to create something new and you have to be able to sell it. In England, higher education is now under the Ministry of Business and Innovation. This ever-changing, increasingly complex material culture requires an industrial-scale educational system to provide the skills and disciplines to support it, and children are being co-opted into the system at an earlier and earlier age.

The financial district has replaced the cathedral at the centre of our cities, where the banks take pride of place, soaring ever upwards in their skyscrapers. Without the transformation in banking, the modern world would not have been possible. However, it was to be within the modern system that banking would mutate and become a world in itself, creating money out of thin air and in ways that are becoming more and more difficult to comprehend – banking has morphed into a weird kind of materialistic mysticism. The holy of holies of the modern system is the stock market. If it goes up, it's heaven, and if it goes down, it's hell; growth is everything. Today, in order for the modern system to keep growing, it is having to go deeper and deeper into debt. After many financial crises, some economists are predicting that the system cannot survive.

Commerce has restructured our way of life, which is now divided between work and leisure. Work is highly organized, disciplined and takes up most of our time. Leisure belongs to us, we have earned it and can spend it as we wish. We can become a football fan, follow our favourite band every weekend, watch movies or play video games as much as we like. We can answer the call of the travel agent to visit some new paradise resort during our short breaks from the work place - our holidays, which in Christendom were holy days. Paradise is now on earth, until it is spoilt by too many visitors. We can go and observe our fellow creatures living in reserves, removed from their disappearing habitats and cut off from us. We can go and study any number of dead and dying cultures and civilisations in our museums, eat food from anywhere in the world and, if religiously inclined, worship any way we like. This is our right, but it belongs to our private world of leisure and has nothing to do with the work place. The centres where we meet and celebrate our togetherness are no longer the places of worship, they are the shopping malls.

The modern system, however, faces a major problem in turning the human being into a consumer: humanity is created for the long duration. In normal times, most people would remain in their places of birth throughout their lives, deeply attached to their particular environments. They would live in their extended families and communities from the cradle to the grave, forging deep and lasting relationships. What were called heirlooms, meaning treasured possessions handed down through generations, meant that nothing was thrown away, everything was mended until it was worn out. Through their religion and way of life, people were part of the natural cycles and rhythms of day and week, month and year.

But to create the consumer, the long duration had to be supplanted by the short duration. The short duration, with that rush of adrenalin which accompanies excitement, a surprise arrival, an anticipated event, a shock or fleeing from danger, has to become the norm so that the individual will always crave the new experience and sensation. The heirloom must be replaced by the disposable product to keep the machines running. All restraints must be lifted from the individual so that pure desire can be released and the perfect consumer created.

The modern way of life has produced an environment that has turned night into day and shattered communities and the extended family, reducing the basis of society to the nuclear family. The nuclear family is highly unstable and often ends with the single parent family. However, it is the change that is taking place to childhood that is most radical.

Childhood is a great mystery. Up until the age of around seven, children live in their own worlds. Neuroscientists have noticed that at this time a change takes place in the brain. Traditionally it was after the age of seven that the child began to be educated. It is amazing how little we can remember of our early childhood, and this is for a very good reason. We are spiritual beings and when we arrive in this world, we have our senses and perceive everything directly through them. We start our lives with pure imaginations and live in the moment. Children playing together can conjure up anything, they can turn a tree trunk into a magnificent carriage and a stick into a sword, they can become pirates or princes. In normal environments children would be able to roam, with older children leading the younger. As children grew, they would pass through the stages of being led and becoming leader, and experience the joys, frustrations and miseries of interacting with their peers. Games would be full of laughter and crying, tragedy, adventure and comedy. The community would provide the boundaries for their roaming and would only intervene when things got out of hand. This roaming, communal childhood allowed children to grow naturally and develop their own imaginations and personalities, and to form friendships that would last a lifetime.

But the modern cult requires us to be transformed into consumers and this can only be achieved if childhood is re-engineered. The child must be conditioned to live in the short duration, and to achieve this a consumer childhood has to be invented. So, marketeers created their version of childhood. Plastic toys in garish colours, leaving nothing to the imagination, are placed before the child. The child is excited by this apparition, plays with it for a while and then gets bored. To keep the child happy, the toy is replaced by another and then another, and so it goes on until the child develops an addictive personality. The imagination is further assailed by films and games that completely hypnotize the child. Robbed of his/her own imagination, the child becomes dependent on an external source, and a dialysis of the imagination takes over. And now the Kantian nightmare kicks in. The child is immersed and surrounded by the images and ideology of the sovereignty of the individual, and is being taught from an early age that he or she must think for himself or herself, yet without any personal development having been achieved nor any objective criteria attained.

Prematurely wrenched out of childhood with their identities malformed, the children become self-obsessed and regard the world with the eyes of consumers; everything now becomes a matter of personal choice. By the time of reaching the next major transition in the teenage years, the child rebels. Deprived of roaming and the formation of proper relationships in their own world of childhood, the transitioning children now attempt to create their own society separate from the adults, just when the relationship between the adult and the child is most important in drawing the child into adulthood. What has followed is brilliantly described in Robert Bly's *Sibling Society*. Instead of a vertical social structure where the different stages of life are linked, it turns into a layered horizontal society, where each generation is forever trapped in an arrested adolescence.

The hegemony of the merchant has turned human society into an appetite that can never be satisfied and is literally devouring the world.

5

ART & THE ENVIRONMENT

ISLAM

AL-GHAZĀLĪ REFERS to the wisdom of the craftsman, and it is through the elevation of the senses that craftsmen participated in the synthesis of knowledge. Just as the sharia enshrined the way of life for the Muslim, the craftsmen fashioned the environment in which the Islamic way of life could be lived. The sharia and the Islamic city came into being organically and in parallel. New settlements were formed by the Arab armies, which were stationed outside the great centres of population, and these settlements grew into cities, the most famous being Kufa, Kairouan and Fustat. The most important building in the city was the great mosque, adjacent to which were the markets and then the various neighbourhoods. Each neighbourhood had its mosque and public baths. Institutes of learning grew up around the mosques, while around the markets, workshops, warehouses and hostels for travelling merchants were located.

The city was like a beehive, with narrow lanes connecting the various parts. It was an environment in which the exterior was simple and the interior of mosques and homes full of light and beauty, mirroring the ideal for the believer of living a simple outer life and a rich inner life. Shoes were removed on entering the mosque and the home, creating a clear demarcation between the bustle of the exterior world and the peace and tranquillity of the inner sanctum of the family, and of the community at prayer.

This model of the city transformed the existing historic centres and spread across Afro-Eurasia as Dār al-Islām expanded. Today, it can still be experienced in what remains of the traditional cities of Islam.

Although the formation of Islamic art took time, the fundamental principles of Islamic architecture were already manifest in the Dome of the Rock in Jerusalem, built within sixty years of the death of the Prophet. The Umayyad Caliph ʿAbd al-Malik received from the Byzantine Emperor the gift of hundreds of craftsmen who constructed this building, the first to fully express the Islamic aesthetic. The late architectural model maker, Kim Allen, in his work on the Dome of the Rock explained how in its geometry it contains perfect balance, which had not been realised in preceding Byzantine edifices. This balance between the vertical and the horizontal would become a feature of the mosque, in contrast to the Gothic cathedral with its accent on the vertical. However, the decoration of the Dome of the Rock that we see today is much later. The Umayyad Mosque in Damascus, built a few years after the Dome of the Rock, still displays mosaics of scenes drawn from nature, which were completed at the time.

It was not until more than two hundred years later that the calligrapher Ibn Muqla standardised the forms of calligraphy which, when integrated within geometric pattern and arabesque, perfectly express the concept of unity at the heart of the Islamic Revelation, and, in its architectural setting, ensured that the Islamic environment was free of naturalistic images, averting the danger of descending into the glorification of the human form. The beauty of the objects of daily life served to elevate simple acts such as washing and eating, while the pleasure of conversation was embellished with poetry and stories. A rich and fulfilling theatre of life made the separate art of the theatre obsolete. Life, from the cradle to the grave, was the play and the whole society formed the cast.

Surrounding the city and integrated within it were the orchards and gardens which provided the food and were also places of recreation and refreshment. The Qur'an and the Hadith of the Prophet instilled in Muslims as they tended nature a profound respect for the Creator and mankind's relationship with His creation:

> *Have you considered what you cultivate? Is it you that causes it to grow, or do We cause it to grow?* (Qur'an, 56:63-64)

> *And the earth He laid out for [His] creatures, wherein is fruit, and palm trees having sheaths, and grain with husks, and fragrant herbs. So which of the favours of your Lord would you deny? (Qur'an, 55:10-13)*

> *Never does a Muslim plant a tree or cultivate land from which man, bird or beast eats, but that he is rewarded for it as an act of charity.* (Bukhārī and Muslim)

The Prophet's own love and care for the natural world is captured in many hadith:

> *When the Prophet saw a donkey had been branded on its face, he said, 'Have you not heard that I have cursed anyone who brands an animal on its face or hits it on its face?'* (Muslim)

> *Abū Hurayra narrated that the Prophet said: 'A man saw a dog eating mud out of thirst, so the man took his shoe and used it to pour water for the dog until the dog's thirst was quenched. God thanked him and admitted him to Paradise.'* (Bukhārī and Muslim)

Within the world of Islam there was a prodigious dissemination of trees, plants and crops. Yemeni and Syrian farmers turned Andalusia into a garden, introducing water management systems that brought to life an arid landscape. The development that took place in husbandry is captured in a number of scholarly works known as the Filāha Texts. In them we see traditional agriculture developing so that large urban centres could be supported in a sustainable manner that worked in collaboration with nature. This development of agriculture mirrored the increase in the founding of cities which accompanied the spread of Islam.

The courts of the rulers both enabled, and were transformed by, the evolution in the crafts and husbandry. Palaces became centres of the finest craftsmanship and contained the most advanced and beautiful walled gardens. These gardens mixed ornamental and productive plants and trees. The quality of craftsmanship and husbandry produced in the courts was disseminated throughout the society. The courts were also centres for the patronage of poets and musicians, who contributed to the refinement of princes and the further civilising of society. An ancient genre of literature, the 'Mirrors for Princes', was adopted and developed to teach the rulers how to govern wisely, helping to educate many great sultans who advanced, maintained and protected Islamic civilisation.

Once again, we turn to the traveller, Ibn Battūta, to give us a first-hand illustration of the harmonious city environment of merchants, husbandmen and craftsman that we have been describing. Here, in the translation of Gibb and Beckingham, Ibn Battūta gives us a picture of Damascus in the 14th century:

> Damascus … is an exceedingly noble, glorious, and beauteous city, rich in all manner of merchandise, and everywhere delightful, … abounding in foods, spices, precious stones, silk, pearls, cloth-of-gold, perfumes from India, Tartary, Egypt, Syria, and places on our side of the Mediterranean, and in all precious things the heart of man can conceive. It is begirt with gardens and orchards, is watered both within and without by rivers, brooks, and fountains, cunningly arranged, to minister to men's luxury, and is incredibly populous, being inhabited by divers trades of most skillful and noble workmen, craftsmen, and merchants, while within the walls it is adorned beyond belief by baths, by birds that sing all the year around, and by pleasures, refreshments, and amusements of all kinds.

THE WEST

THE CHRISTIAN ENVIRONMENT was dominated by the great cathedrals and abbeys, which towered above the world that surrounded them. Every art and craft was utilised in the creation and beautification of these houses of God. Sculptures, paintings and stained-glass windows, depicting the stories of the Bible and the lives of the saints, accompanied by the chanting of the choir, created an awesome setting for the congregation to worship and glorify their Creator. Craftsmen and women working in wood, textiles, gold and other metals, produced the furnishings, garments and alter pieces, and the lecterns on which the beautifully illuminated bibles rested. The nativity and passion of Christ were brought to life in plays, enacted on stages erected in front of the churches, in which the whole community of priests, nobles and peasants participated, either as performers or audience.

The Reformation divided Europe religiously, but the Renaissance was adopted by both branches of Christianity in different ways. Whereas the Catholics largely absorbed the new movement and used the naturalism of Renaissance art in the service of the religion, the Protestants made a clear divide between religion and culture, between the sacred and the secular, and nowhere more so than in England. With the destruction of the monasteries in the 16th century, Henry VIII not only demolished the thousand-year practice of contemplation at the heart of Christianity, but also erased much of the Christian artistic and cultural heritage.

With the Renaissance, in both the Catholic and Protestant worlds, a fundamental change took place in the status of the artist and the nature of art itself. Until now the artist had belonged to a guild, which enjoyed similar status to all the other craft guilds, and, in the service of the Church, they had joined together to produce sanctuaries of sublime beauty. But now, it was to be the artist who would be responsible for manifesting the glorification of the human. The Renaissance artist was renamed and became the 'artificer', a term in Latin that had been used in theology to denote God as Creator. The term genius also changed its meaning; in ancient Rome the genius was the guardian spirit or tutelary deity of a person, now it became a part of the very soul of the person. Vasari, the famous art historian of the time, spoke of Michelangelo as a divine genius.

Michelangelo was considered to have surpassed the ancients. He had even surpassed nature. His Pieta was so full of human pathos that it appeared to be alive. The 'work of art' was born, with its creator the 'fine artist', as distinct from the artist-craftsman. The portrait was considered to be the highest form of fine art, capturing the soul of the individual human being. Also favoured by art collectors through to the 19th century were the classical myths and stories of ancient Greece and Rome. The French artist David, in his painting of the death of Socrates, brilliantly depicts the different kinds of emotions expressed by the disciples surrounding the great philosopher, as he calmly approaches his end.

Academies of fine arts were founded in Florence (1563), Paris (1648), London (1768) and many other cities throughout Europe and the West. Following on from the Greeks and Romans, and fundamentally contradicting the Christian code, the new humanist valued the beauty and perfection of the naked human form above everything in art, and what became known as life drawing took pride of place amongst the skills that students needed to acquire. The annual exhibition became the most important place for the artist's work to be seen.

In architecture, Vitruvius, the Roman writer who had meticulously recorded the principles and methods of Roman architecture, became the great authority and his work the bible for the new movement, which was transforming town and cityscape. The villages and towns of Christian Europe had grown organically, with winding streets and every house unique in its design. By contrast, the new 'civilised' environment was planned from outside, with its orderly squares and crescents, identical terraced houses and lines of parallel avenues. The design for the various decorative elements were taken from pattern books, and there was little scope for the craftsman's imagination.

Having come under the spell of this new aesthetic, the architecture belonging to the world that had been abandoned was found to be ugly and called 'Gothic', referring to the barbaric Germanic tribes known as the Goths. So, if it was not possible to build anew, a classical front to cover up the offending view would be constructed. However, in England, the opportunity for the new movement to take centre stage came with the fire of London (1666), which gutted St Paul's Cathedral and most of the city's churches. The cathedral and all the damaged churches were rebuilt in the classical style.

It was another fire in London 168 years later, when the Houses of Parliament were burnt down, that presaged the return of Gothic architecture in the rebuilding of the seat of Government. This was the result of the 19th century revival of Christianity in England that demanded a Christian architecture. What was named the Battle of Styles took place between the supporters of the classical and the Gothic. After a time, the animosity faded and architects mastered both styles, mainly using Gothic for ecclesiastical buildings, and classical for secular edifices. The Houses of Parliament brought the styles together, it has a classical frame with Gothic decoration. Christianity and classical civilisation had found a way of co-existing, despite their contradictions, and would continue to build their mixed environment well into the twentieth century. This accommodation would allow the entry of a third member, modern architecture.

By the beginning of the twentieth century, industrialisation had transformed northern Europe.

Bridges spanned mighty rivers, railway stations were larger than cathedrals and trains were travelling under capital cities in tunnels. New materials allowed architects to do practically anything. The modern movement first developed in Germany and France, where certain architects could see a contradiction between the world that was being born, and architecture that belonged to another age. They were excited by the possibilities that had been opened up by industrialisation. They wished for a clean slate on which to create a new world, free of the baggage of the past.

Le Corbusier's declaration that 'a house is a machine for living in', resonated with a new generation of architects who began to give expression to this new machine age that would be completely at odds with everything that had preceded it. In the world before the Industrial Revolution, architects and craftsmen everywhere created their environments out of the materials around them. These materials imposed natural limits, and it is out of these limitations and the skill of the craftsman that the beauty that is typical of traditional architecture, from the most sophisticated of urban structures to the simplest of village dwellings, was created. Once these limitations were breached, the balance between the craftsman and his materials was broken and the chaos of the modern environment unleashed.

When I was born in 1942, the population of the world was around two billion; when I reached seventy, it was passing seven billion. More than half the world's built environment has been constructed in the last thirty years. With the industrialisation of agriculture and the rapid increase in factories, the movement of populations from rural to urban escalated, and around the year 2010 more than 50% of the world's population had become urban, with many thousands joining the daily migration. This has led to mega-cities of up to twenty million residents, urban jungles that are choked with pollution. For centuries, the population remained remarkably stable and it only needed a 2% change of life over death to cause the population explosion. The population continues to increase, and much of the environment is now modern in structure and design. Only pockets are left of what existed before, and these have mostly been adapted to conform to the new modern way of life. It is a bleak, soulless and dehumanised landscape that now surrounds most of humanity.

But what of the fine artist in this new commercial world? Two quite different paths opened up for them. The first was the world of advertising. Artists were commandeered, and used their considerable skills to demonstrate the wonders of products, in order to convince the public that they could not possibly live without them. Brilliantly designed, their logos and branding became a familiar part of the environment. The car became a symbol of freedom. You could be transported anywhere by airplane to discover and enjoy the world and, using the products of the burgeoning beauty industry, you too could be ever-young and beautiful.

The other path for the fine artist continued the idea of the work of fine art that had emerged in the Renaissance. By the middle of the nineteenth century, artists were beginning to rebel against their establishment. The Académie des Beaux Arts in Paris was the upholder of the principles and methods of the classical fine arts. Their standards were rigorously maintained in their annual exhibition, the Salon de Paris. The rebels were tired of the artificiality and endless repetition of the same subjects. They viewed perspective and other traditional techniques as straight-jackets that stifled their creativity. They wanted to paint the world around them as they saw it, express their own feelings and emotions in the paintings, and be free to develop their own methods. They had tuned into the spirit of the modern age and were driven by the desire to create something new, to be renowned for their originality.

But these artists had not only rebelled against the art establishment, they had turned their backs on the morality and way of life of bourgeois society, wishing to live by their own rules. Rejected by the Academy, they sought refuge in the poorest quarters of Paris, where music-hall entertainers, circus people, prostitutes and other undesirables lived. True to their beliefs, they were prepared to suffer and starve in pursuit of their art, and many of them suffered terribly. An outraged society created a new name for them; they were called 'bohemians', the abusive name used for gypsies.

I have likened what became known as the modern artist to the canary in the mine. Miners used to take a canary into the mine and one of the miners was responsible for watching the bird. If it fell off its perch, he would sound the alarm, and the miners would escape with their lives. The canary had detected lethal gas; the bird's life had been sacrificed to warn the miners of the danger. The modern artist, like the canary, is both hyper-sensitive and a warner.

As the nineteenth century turned into the war-stricken twentieth century, a giant emerged. Picasso experienced and expressed the cruelty, chaos and disintegration of this new century as it unfolded. His shattering of the image in his painting of the prostitutes of the Rue d'Avignon was shocking, and even his modernist colleagues were outraged at the time, believing that he was ridiculing the movement. However, he was the trailblazer, and they would come to hail the painting as a masterpiece. When Hitler's planes bombed Guernica during the Spanish Civil

War, the first such blitzing of an urban centre, he was grief stricken and produced a painting that graphically expressed the full horror and barbaric cruelty of the event. However, it was through his relationship with the feminine that Picasso's mastery as an artist and his self-obsession and cruelty as a man were fully realised. He had been classically trained and could turn his hand to anything, and as each relationship began, it heralded a new period of creativity. He once stated that women were of two kinds, goddesses and doormats. To begin with, each one was a muse for him, but once the aura faded, they had to be replaced to keep the flame of creativity burning. He left in his wake great suffering and tragedy in the lives of his women and children. Born a Catholic, he lost his faith in God and became a Marxist. But throughout his life he was obsessed with death, and as his own end approached, terror enveloped him, brilliantly captured in the final of the thousands of self-portraits he painted during his lifetime.

Francis Bacon cited Picasso as his reason for becoming an artist. As a young man he had been turned down by the army at the beginning of the second world war for health reasons, and had volunteered for the team that went into the bombed-out areas of London during the Blitz to recover the dead and dying. His sensitive artist's soul was traumatised. He lived in a haze of alcohol and sadomasochism and out of this depraved and tormented man came the melting, dissolving, distorted, hideous images of his art.

Jackson Pollock was a sensitive and a deeply disturbed soul. He penetrated through to the chaos of the world behind the glossy image of the American dream, and expressed the chaos through his art. The accumulating chaos passing through his soul turned his life into chaos. At the age of forty-four, he drove his car at one hundred miles an hour, crashed into a tree and was killed.

Eduardo Paolozzi shows how we humans are being transformed into robots, while Tracy Emin represents the Twitter generation and the Freudian idea that anything we have inside us is worth sharing. One of her works consists of a tent in which she has exhibited the names of all those she ever slept with.

Damien Hirst comes from a working-class Catholic family. His parents divorced when he was a child, and as a divorcee his mother was refused the sacrament of communion. He lost his faith and became an atheist. In his art he delivers a chilling message, which might be described as 'death without redemption', the atheist's vision of death. In one of his works he shows us the life cycle of the fly. Maggots hatch on the head of a cow, and after a brief life are incinerated by an electric zapper that hangs above the cow's head.

These artists have been the chroniclers of the horrors of the twentieth century as it unfolded. Their works are warnings to society. But instead of heeding the warnings, society has turned them into objects of celebration, glorifying them as great works of art, and elevating them to the status of icons. The Christian artists glorified God through their work. The classical artists celebrated great men and elevating myths. In the world of the merchant the work of art itself has become the thing of value. A triptych by Bacon was auctioned for $130 million; one of Jackson Pollock's paintings was sold for $170 million; Damien Hirst's studio of new works was auctioned for more than $100 million, and Picasso's Guernica is beyond price.

The canaries in the mines did not know the reasons for their deaths. The modern artists, bereft of tradition and malformed, may not realise that what they are carrying is the ugly reflection of a cruel, depraved, chaotic, robotic, shallow, empty world, for they are in love with their creations, and believe in them as great works of art. The modern artist rebelled against the classical tradition of art, but not against the idea of the artist as the divine genius and creator. A cult has formed around them, a parody of Christ and the church. The artist is the Christ figure, whose work is mediated through the critic, who plays the role of the high priest explaining its meaning to a bewildered congregation. The patrons of the cult are the collectors, and they are served by the dealers and auctioneers. The summit is reached, in this strange world, with the canonisation of the artist through the retrospective exhibition, when the artist joins the immortals.

Damien Hirst was canonised in 2012 with his retrospective at Tate Modern. The exhibition displayed many variations on the theme that I have called death without redemption; dead butterflies arranged like a kaleidoscope, boxes of pills, cigarette ends, dead fish, pills laid out on glass shelves, and surgical instruments accompanied by a full skeleton. The centrepiece was a human skull covered in £50 million worth of diamonds, housed in its own shrine. People queued for up to three hours to stand in front of it for a few minutes. Money and death, that was the message. The modern artist now mirrors the essence of modernity, revealing its absurdity; you must create something new and you must be able to sell it; innovation and entrepreneurship. Damien Hirst has been very successful achieving this.

Modern art is now being housed in buildings that are designed to be in perpetual states of disequilibrium, perfectly mirroring what is inside them, and these buildings are appearing all over the world. This brings me to what, I believe, is the most alarming aspect relating to modern art. The modern artist rebelled against the established order, and became an outsider. Now the modern artist is at the heart of the establishment. The natural instinct of the general public is to recoil from their creations, but because the establishment honours them and celebrates their work, resistance evaporates. The influence of modern art is spreading throughout society and the world, and is now playing a key role in the perpetuation of the modern cult. It is programming us to be able to live in a state of chaos, to love ugliness, to enjoy disequilibrium; it is normalising the abnormal.

One of the processes by which this aberrational world has come into being is through the shock of something that is outrageous entering the mainstream. In his book *The Prince*, Machiavelli enshrined the idea that the end justifies the means and that, 'Politics has no relation to morals'. Bernard de Mandeville (d. 1733) in his *Fable of the Bees* promoted vice over virtue:

> Then leave Complaints; Fools only strive
> To make a Great and Honest Hive.
> T'enjoy the World's Conveniences,
> Be famed in War, but live in Ease.
> Without great Vices, is a vain
> Eutopia seated in the Brain.

Picasso's painting *Les Demoiselles d'Avignon* and Germaine Greer's book *The Female Eunuch* were both shocking and unacceptable when they first appeared, but then became normalised and finally celebrated.

Now, as the escalating and multiplying crises are flooding into the gilded cage of our own making, we watch helplessly as the human tragedy unfolds, and the earth and all the living creatures upon it, groan under our weight.

6
CONQUEST & EXPANSION

ISLAM

THE SPEED OF THE CONQUEST which laid the foundations of Islamic civilisation has always amazed historians. Within a generation of the Prophet's death, the Umayyad Empire stretched from Spain to the borders of India and China. These lands contained many different cultures and civilisations with established traditions, long recorded histories and deeply held beliefs, but conquest did not imply the imposition of Islam upon people of other faiths, as is indicated by the Qur'anic verse that forbids forced conversion:

> *There is no compulsion in religion; right guidance is clearly distinct from error. Whoever rejects false deities and believes in God has grasped the firmest handhold that never breaks. And God is the All-hearing, the All-knowing.* (Qur'an, 2:256)

This prohibition of compulsion is related to the way in which the Qur'an continually emphasises that in inviting to Islam, the Muslim should appeal to people's intelligence:

> *Invite to the way of your Lord with wisdom and fair admonition, and argue with them in the best way.* (Qur'an,16:125).

Moreover, the Qur'an teaches that all the worlds that preceded Islam had received Revelation:

> *...For each of you We have established a law and a way; and if God had willed, He would have made you one people. But [He wanted to] test you in what He has given you. So vie with one another in good works. To God you shall all return, and He will inform you about that in which you differed.* (Qur'an, 5:48)

The Western idea that Islam was spread by the sword has been thoroughly discredited by the evidence, and is an example of placing upon Islam what actually happened in Christianity. Islam spread in various ways, but rarely by compulsion. People were attracted by the simplicity of the way of life and the example of pious Muslims. The success of Islam as an empire was also attractive to those with ambition, and living in close contact with Muslims meant that friendships were formed and marriages contracted. The conversion to Islam by members of different communities took place over several centuries, and it is worth bearing in mind that for a long time Muslims were minority rulers. The treatment of conquered peoples of other faiths, who were called *dhimmi*s, had clearly set-out guidelines. Non-Muslims were not required to pay *zakāt* but they did have to pay a special tax known as *jizya*, according to their means. Women, children, the sick and elderly, as well as monks, slaves and the poor were exempt from paying, as were those who served in the military. In exchange for the *jizya*, the non-Muslims were accorded protection, freedom of worship and jurisdiction over their own affairs.

The Muslim belief that the Qur'an with its Messenger was the final and most complete revelation from God to all humanity, was accompanied by the clear understanding that all the worlds the Muslims encountered had a divine origin and, even in their present states, still contained valuable wisdom and knowledge. Ancient civilisations could continue to exist, fully preserved, living alongside and participating in the new civilisation.

One of the most important principles in the spread of Islamic civilisation is the maxim in the sharia that 'custom has the power of law' (*al-ʿādda muhakkama*).

This enabled wisdom, aesthetic preferences and everyday customs of a locality, that were in conformity with the revelation, to be incorporated into the sharia.

> *Wisdom is as lost property to the believer – he may take it wherever he finds it.* (Tirmidhī)

It also produced a built environment that was rooted in the locality and yet fully integrated and belonging to Dār al-Islām. This was a marriage of unity and diversity, and an indication of the universality of Islam.

This universality was also expressed in the relationship of equality between the different peoples and races, which is clearly stated in the Prophet's final sermon:

> *An Arab has no superiority over a non-Arab, nor a non-Arab any superiority over an Arab [...] a white person has no superiority over a black person, nor a black person any superiority over a white person, except in piety and good action.* (Imam Ahmad)

Warfare is an inevitable aspect of human society, and determining the conditions that justify warfare and military practice that are acceptable to Islam was a major concern for Muslim scholars and those engaged in jurisprudence. The Qur'an addresses the subject in a number of passages:

> *Permission is given to those who fight because they have been wronged, and God is indeed able to give them victory; those who have been driven from their homes unjustly only because they said, 'Our Lord is God' – for had it not been for God's repelling some men by means of others, monasteries, churches, synagogues and mosques, in which the name of God is much mentioned, would certainly have been destroyed...*(Qur'an, 22:39-40)

> *Fight in the way of God against those who fight against you, but do not initiate hostilities. Indeed! God does not love aggressors.* (Qur'an, 2:190)

Many hadith give guidance regarding the ethics of war:

> *Do not destroy villages and towns, do not spoil cultivated fields and gardens, and do not slaughter cattle.* (Sahīh Bukhārī; Sunan Abu Dāwūd)

> *No one may punish with fire except the Lord of Fire.* (Sunan Abū Dāwūd)

A famous oration by the first Caliph, Abū Bakr, to his troops emphasises the responsibilities of Muslims in battle:

> *'Stop, O people, that I might provide you with ten rules, that you might be guided in the battlefield. Do not commit treachery or deviate from the right path. Do not mutilate dead bodies. Neither kill a child, nor a woman, nor an aged man. Bring no harm to the trees, nor burn them with*

> *fire, especially fruit trees. Do not kill any of the enemy's flock, save for your own food alone. It is likely you will pass by people who have devoted their lives to monasticism; leave them be.'* (Tabarī)

The care taken to protect monasteries was illustrated when Sultan Mehmet, the conqueror of Constantinople, had his troops secure the area around Mount Athos, on which many monasteries were situated. The Sultan's wife then presented the monks with an icon from Syria. A very different situation occurred when the 4th Crusade was diverted to Byzantium and the Catholics ransacked the monasteries.

The sharia engaged in every aspect relating to warfare and the cessation of hostilities. Many works were written by scholars from the 9th century onwards covering every area of Islamic military jurisprudence, including: the law of treaties; the treatment of diplomats, hostages, refugees and prisoners of war; the right of asylum; conduct on the battlefield; the protection of women, children and non-combatant civilians; contracts across the lines of battle; the prohibition of the use of certain weapons; and rules regarding damage to the environment.

The arts of battle and codes of chivalry were cultivated by the warriors of Islam. Many great warriors, such as Salāhuddīn Ayyūbī, were revered for their prowess and celebrated in literature. The Spanish author Vicente Blasco reflected that:

> Europe did not know chivalry, or its adopted literature or sense of honour before the arrival of Arabs in Andalusia and the wide[spread] presence of their knights and heroes in the countries of the south.

The strength of Islamic civilisation was tested when the nomadic Turks and Mongols conquered the central lands of Islam, destroying Baghdad, the seat of the Caliphate, in 1258. This seeming disaster, in fact, set in motion a diaspora of scholars and craftsmen and accelerated the spread of Islam to its furthest limits. It also culminated in the conversion of the Turks and Mongols, who provided the ruling dynasties for the following centuries. The Afro-Eurasian world now returned to its pre-Islamic structure of the East Roman Empire, Persia, India and China, with Islam dominating the first three worlds and deeply affecting Chinese civilisation.

In his seminal work *Trade and Civilisation in the Indian Ocean – an Economic History from the Rise of Islam to 1750*, KN Chaudhuri shows how the Muslims played a key role in maintaining and developing the collaborative and peaceful nature of trade and exchange that was the norm between the various cultures and civilisations of Asia, and how the entrance of the Portuguese, and then the other European nations, caused massive disruption, turning it into an arena of perpetual competition and warfare.

The European conquests have cast a shroud over the extraordinary world that preceded it; for the previous thousand years, Islamic civilisation had provided a unifying structure in which the civilisations across Afro-Eurasia could collaborate and participate. To a far greater degree than in previous worlds, Islamic society encouraged travel and was highly mobile. Pilgrims travelling to Mecca, merchants engaged in long distance trade, scholars seeking knowledge and craftsmen looking for work, all travelled the routes of Afro-Eurasia, from the Atlantic to the Pacific, and could expect and would receive hospitality wherever they found themselves. These networks of pilgrimage, trade, knowledge and craft engaged with, and connected into, the various cultures and civilisations, both within and outside Dār al-Islām, transcending empires and states, and producing a world where trade, ideas and technologies flowed freely.

In stories told in the Thousand and One Nights, the reader, or as it would have been the listener, might be seamlessly conveyed from Baghdad to China. And this mirrored the reality: during the first half of the 15th century the Ming Emperor dispatched several great armadas into the Indian Ocean in order to trade and assert China's centrality and authority over the world. These armadas were led by the Chinese Muslim admiral Zheng He, and contained Chinese Muslim merchants and Chinese Muslim scribes to record the voyages, one of which included a pilgrimage to Mecca. But no territory was conquered, the trade routes were not disrupted and the armadas returned peacefully to China, enhancing the reputation of the Celestial Empire.

The relationship between Islam and China was dynamic and multi-faceted; the Mongols brought Persian architects to build Beijing and Chinese artists to their courts in Persia; the decorative arts of China were profoundly affected by Muslim craftsmanship, as observed by Owen Jones in his ground-breaking work *The Grammar of Chinese Ornament*, published in 1867:

> We are led to think that this art must have had in some way a foreign origin; it so nearly resembles in all its principles the art of the Mohammedan races, that we may presume it was derived from them. It would be no difficult task to take a work of ornament of this class, and, by simply varying the colouring and correcting the drawing, convert it into an Indian or Persian composition.

Having received knowledge and skills from the ancient worlds in building their civilisation, now, in return, all the worlds either within or bordering Dār al-Islām were enriched by this new creation. Christian and Jewish communities participated in the culture, as did Hindus and Buddhists in India, with Arabic, Persian, Turkish and Urdu becoming the languages of civilised discourse. So great was the attraction of this culture in Islamic Spain that it elicited this lament from a Christian prelate:

> My Christian brothers admire the poetry and chivalry stories of the Arabs, and they study the books written by the philosophers and scholars of the Muslims. They do not do that in order to refute them, but rather to learn the eloquent Arabic style. Where today – apart from the clergy – are those who read the religious commentaries on the Old and New Testaments? Alas, the new generation of intelligent Christians do not know any literature and language well, apart from Arabic literature and the Arabic language. They avidly read the books of the Arabs and amass huge libraries of these books at great expense.

Sufism had a profound impact on all the religious worlds, which in many other ways were enriched by their connection to Islamic civilisation. Indeed, one of the greatest beneficiaries was Western Christendom, which as we have already noted, was both intellectually and materially enriched.

The way that Jews were treated by the Muslims was very different from the treatment they received from the Christians, and this is clearly illustrated during the momentous events of the second half of the 15th century. Rabbi Yitzhak Safarti, the Chief Rabbi of the city of Edirne, sent out a letter to the Jewish communities of Europe soon after the fall of the

Byzantine Empire in 1453, inviting his co-religionists to leave the torments that they were enduring in Christendom and to seek safety and prosperity in Turkey. In 1492, Queen Isabella and King Ferdinand of Spain expelled the Jews from their country, which along with the Spanish Inquisition that followed, was arguably one of the most traumatic events in Jewish history prior to the Holocaust. That same year, Sultan Bayezid II issued a proclamation ordering his officials to accept the Sephardic Jews into his country. Around 250,000 Jews came to settle in Ottoman lands, with most heading towards Istanbul and Thessalonica, which absorbed a total of 100,000 Jews. Thessalonica remained for centuries a thriving centre of Jewish culture until World War Two when it was destroyed by the Holocaust.

A further insight into the rich pre-modern relationship between Muslims and Jews is to be found in the Cairo Genizah collection of some 200,000 texts held in the Cambridge University Library. These go back a thousand years and cover many aspects of the life of the Jewish community. They reveal Muslims and Jews collaborating in long-distance trading ventures. Among the texts is the record of a dispute which divided the Jewish community in Cairo when the son of the great philosopher Maimonides was their leader. The dispute was resolved by the Mufti of

Cairo, the Muslim religious leader at the time, who was invited to arbitrate between the sides. For most of its history under Islam, Jewish culture flourished; Jews fully participated in trade and the crafts, were famous as physicians, and played a prominent role in administration, even providing several viziers, the highest position under the sultan. Jewish communities were woven into the fabric of the world of Islam. Today, it is difficult to appreciate the harmony that for the most part existed between Muslims and Jews when Islam dominated the Afro-Eurasian world.

The same lack of understanding exists regarding Islam in Africa south of the Sahara, and the amazing transformation that took place. Islam was carried to this distant region by merchants attracted by the most extensive gold deposits known at the time. But it was Mansa Mūsā, the Sultan of Mali, whose pilgrimage to Mecca in 1325 quite literally put this part of Africa on the map and turned him into a legend; he is depicted in a Catalan Atlas of 1375, seated on his throne holding a gold coin. The 16th century Malian historian Mahmud Kati in his *Chronicle of the Seekers* places Mansa Mūsā's pilgrimage in context:

> From the far reaches of the Mediterranean Sea to the Indus River, the faithful approached the city of Mecca. All had the same objective: to worship together at the most sacred shrine of Islam, the Kaaba in Mecca. One such traveller

> was Mansa Mūsā, Sultan of Mali in Western Africa. Mansa Mūsā had prepared carefully for the long journey he and his attendants would take. He was determined to travel not only for his own religious fulfillment, but also for recruiting teachers and leaders, so that his realms could learn more of the Prophet's teachings.

Western accounts have focused on his fabulous wealth, describing how his caravan of sixty thousand men was like a city on the move, a city whose inhabitants, all the way down to the slaves, were clad in gold brocade and finest Persian silk. A hundred camels were in tow, each camel carrying hundreds of pounds of pure gold.

However, it was what he brought back with him that had lasting significance. He gathered together scholars and artisans, including the Andalusian poet and architect Abū Ishāq al-Sāhili, whose masterpiece was the famous Djinguereber mosque. Timbuktu was transformed into a great centre of education, with its universities attracting scholars and students from across the world of Islam. The University of Sankore became the most famous of several universities in Timbuktu. It had its roots in the Sankore Mosque which was founded in 980, and is reputed to have had libraries containing a million manuscripts. As well as gold, Timbuktu became famous for the production and copying of books which were exported to North Africa and Egypt.

In recent times, the discovery of hundreds of thousands of manuscripts in private collections, contained in chests found in houses and tents in Mali and across the Sahel, has demonstrated the depth of scholarship that reached into the whole society – city dwellers, villagers and nomads.

During the centuries of Islamic civilisation, slaves came from many quarters, including Africa. Over time they were integrated into the civilisation through the various vocational routes. Travel today from Morocco to Malaysia through all the countries that were under Islam and you will not find the remains of a slave caste as you have in the Americas. In Islam, a child born to a slave woman by a freeman had the same rights as his children born in marriage. The slaves were absorbed into the mainstream of society, many becoming eminent scholars, famous warriors and wealthy merchants.

A fragmented understanding of the past and the jaundiced view of Islam which exist today have meant that the overwhelming impact that Islamic civilisation had upon the world has been little researched and even less understood. Islam's conquest was far reaching, long lasting and enriching, both for those who chose to remain within their historic communities, as well as for those cultures and civilisations neighbouring Dār al-Islām.

THE WEST

THE EUROPEAN CONQUEST of the world can be divided into two periods, with the watershed being the Industrial Revolution. In the first period, the Americas were completely vanquished and the rich sea trade of Asia monopolised. With the Industrial Revolution the pace quickened, the great civilisations of Asia were either conquered or brought under European control, and the vast continent of Africa was shared out between the European nations. A new global structure was formed, with Europe at its centre.

By the 16th century, the newly formed European sovereign states consisted of an exclusive version of Christianity, an idealised civilisation, a company of voracious merchants and a warrior caste honed in the continuous warfare that was becoming endemic in Europe, and increasingly brutal with each new technological development. And these new warlike entities were about to erupt into an unsuspecting world. The sense of superiority which the European now embodied had gone far beyond what was natural to human collectives.

Each nation state was creating its myth of origin, and we can see this taking place in the case of Portugal in Camoes' epic poem *The Lusiads.* It tells the story of the saving of the land of Portugal from the Moors, and Vasco de Gama's triumphant entry into the Indian Ocean. It invokes all the ancient gods as well as Jesus Christ in claiming Portugal and the Portuguese to be the greatest seafaring conquerors the world had ever witnessed, who far surpassed the heroes of the ancients, most of whom only existed in myth. The nobility and courage of the Portuguese and the savagery and cowardice of those they encountered, particularly the Muslims, leaps eloquently from the pages. The reader is left in no doubt that the Portuguese are another breed compared to the rest of humanity, and this over-arching pride in nation was enjoyed by every European state, reaching its summit with the British in India.

Christianity was an exclusive religion with the belief that it was the only way to salvation; all other religions were false. But within Christendom pride in oneself was powerfully controlled through its ethical teachings. With the split in Christendom came certainty concerning one's own version of the Faith, and intolerance and hostility towards the versions followed by others. However, it was the Europeans' approach to civilisation that set them apart from all other cultures and civilisations. Their idealisation of the dead world of Greece and Rome meant that no living civilisation could compare with them. Added to this, the Europeans had become so used to communing with a dead world that they had difficulty in relating to the living. This meant that every culture or civilisation that the Europeans encountered was either completely or partially destroyed and replaced by the European ideal. Their cultural remains were gathered up and placed in museums – mausoleums where they could be preserved and properly studied.

However, at the end of the 15th century the eruption of Europe upon the world stage seemed highly unlikely. Christendom was in retreat before a resurgent Islam. The Holy Land had been lost and the Ottoman Empire had conquered Byzantium, bringing Constantinople under its rule and the Eastern Mediterranean under its control. The only light for the Christians was their conquest of the entire Iberian Peninsula. A new strategy to defeat the Muslims began to form. The Portuguese had for decades been sailing further and further down the west coast of Africa. Their objective was to find a direct route into the Indian Ocean and the great wealth of Asia. It would also enable them to attack Islam from the south and destroy Mecca.

Christopher Columbus had devised another solution to the same problem: to reach India by sailing west.

He took his idea to a number of rulers, including Henry VII of England, but none of them felt inclined to support him. His final visit was to King Ferdinand of Aragon and Queen Isabella of Castile, who were in Granada fighting the Moors. To begin with, they turned him down, but then Granada capitulated. In the euphoria of the moment, they called him back and agreed to fund his venture.

Meanwhile, the Jews were expelled from Spain or forced to convert to Christianity. Whilst the Muslim merchants and courtiers were able to leave, a treaty was agreed allowing the majority of the Muslims, who were the farmers and craftsmen of the south of Spain, to remain and retain their religion. The treaty lasted a very short time and was followed by the imposition of conversion or death, with no possibility of being able to leave Spain. In his seminal work *Blood & Faith,* Matthew Carr relates the little-known story of what finally happened to the Muslims of Spain. By the beginning of the 17th century, Spain's golden age was fading, and the Spanish became obsessed with the doctrine of *Limpieza de Sangre,* 'purity of blood'. In an attempt to revive their flagging kingdom, they expelled all those with Arab or Berber blood, whether they were sincere Christians or only outwardly adhering to Christianity and keeping their Islam secret. After 120 years many had been completely absorbed into Spanish culture, but it did not matter. They had become the scapegoats for a Spain in decline, brilliantly captured in Cervantes' masterpiece *Don Quixote.* In one of the worst events in European history, hundreds of thousands of Moriscos, as they were called, were torn from their homes and sent into exile, many dying on the way. Spain was damaged economically by this act with parts of the South never recovering their former prosperity. Now there were no Muslims in Christian Europe. Only Jewish communities remained, always living in a precarious position, and likely to be persecuted or expelled at any time.

Let us return to Christopher Columbus. In 1492 he landed in the Americas imagining he had arrived in the Indies, and in 1498 Vasco de Gama rounded the Cape of Good Hope and entered the Indian Ocean. The Pope proclaimed the voyages to be crusades, and in the treaty of Tordesillas he divided the world between the Spanish and the Portuguese, giving most of the Americas to the Spanish, save Brazil, and granting Asia to the Portuguese, excepting the Philippines. However, a great surprise awaited them: Islam and thriving Muslim communities were to be found throughout the Indian Ocean and China Sea. Mecca would not be conquered from the south.

The Portuguese came to conquer and convert. For a hundred years they attempted to control and monopolise all the trade of Asia that travelled by sea. To achieve this they acquired, through superior fire-power and strategy, the key ports of Malacca, Macau, Goa and many others. No merchant ship that used their ports or that they encountered on the high seas, was allowed to travel without a permit issued by the

Portuguese authority. If those sailing the ships did not have a permit, they were treated as pirates and their cargo confiscated. A reign of terror existed at sea, and on land the Portuguese carried the Inquisition with them; inhabitants of their port enclaves were forcibly converted to Christianity. This strange empire of the sea, which had all the characteristics of a protection racket, could not last.

By the beginning of the 17th century, the Portuguese were being harried by the great land empires, native shipping was becoming more difficult to control and other European nations were entering the arena. The Portuguese lost their monopoly and many of their ports; those that remained became absorbed into their Asian hinterland, and Portugal began its long decline.

The 17th century belonged to the Dutch. They did not make the mistake that the Portuguese had made by trying to monopolise the system; they focused their efforts on spices, the most valuable of which came from several islands deep in the Malay Archipelago. Led by Jan Pieterszoon Coen, Governor General of the Dutch East India Company, whose rallying call was 'Despair not, spare your enemies not, for God is with us,' they conquered the most important of these islands, killed, deported or enslaved the inhabitants, destroyed the crops on any of the other islands, and created for themselves an absolute monopoly. It has been calculated that the Dutch East India Company was the richest business organisation that has ever existed. Its fleet was greater than those of all the European nations put together, and it had honed its warlike prowess in a hundred years of warfare with the Spanish, from which it had emerged victorious.

During the 17th century, Holland was the richest country in Europe and enjoyed its golden age. But by the 18th century the value of spices had plummeted, as it was found they could be grown in other environments. The Dutch moved to colonise the mainland of what is today Indonesia, and for three hundred years exploited the natural wealth of the Islands, maintaining an iron grip over the inhabitants. The Japanese ousted the Dutch during World War II, only for them to return after the war to reclaim their colony. A war of independence ensued which cost the Indonesians some 200,000 lives, but finally after 400 years they were rid of the Dutch.

The 17th century also saw the arrival in the Indian Ocean of the French and the English. By this time, the rulers of India and China were taking a greater interest in who was carrying their trade by sea. The French and English companies were allowed trading posts and for a hundred and fifty years carried on normal trading to the benefit of both parties. Europe had an insatiable appetite for Indian cotton goods and Chinese silks as well as many other fine products. The Europeans had to trade in currency since they had nothing that the

Asians wanted. The Europeans, however, were awash with gold and silver from the mines in the Americas and the profits from the triangular system of trade, with slaves brought from Africa to the Americas, and crops shipped to an expanding and growing Europe. They also had the considerable profits from the sale of the Asian trade goods in Europe and the Americas.

However, in the 18th century the Mughal Empire, which had been the dominant power in India for two hundred years, began to fall apart. The French and English, who were at war with each other across the world, joined in the battles that ensued. The English won their war against the French in India and North America, and also became the rulers of Bengal, the richest province in India. With Great Britain's ascendancy in India and what had taken place in the Americas, the stage was set for the revolution that would change the world.

But first, we must return to the Americas. The European conquest had been total; superior arms and the diseases the Europeans were carrying wreaked havoc upon the indigenous people and they were decimated. The high civilisations of Inca, Maya and Aztec were reduced to rubble, and their wealth and treasure shipped to Europe. In time, artefacts were placed in museums to be studied. But during that time of destruction, thousands of books were put to the flame as the forced conversion to Christianity took place with the attempt to wipe out all traces of the indigenous systems. Bishop Diego De Landa described the process in 1562:

> We found a large number of books … and, as they contained nothing other than that which was seen as superstition and lies of the devil, we burned them all, which they regretted to an amazing degree, and which caused them much affliction.

The Spanish and Portuguese conquistadors had brought with them the Inquisition. As had been the case with the Muslims in Spain, many conformed outwardly but in private retained their traditional beliefs, some retaining them to this day. The full horror of what had taken place was related by a Dominican Friar, Bartolome de las Casas, in a report to the Spanish King:

> The reason the Christians have murdered on such a vast scale and killed anyone and everyone in their way is purely and simply greed … The reader may ask himself if this is not cruelty and injustice of a kind so terrible that it beggars the imagination … and whether these poor people would not fare far better if they were entrusted to the devils in Hell than they do at the hands of the devils of the New World who masquerade as Christians.

When the British, French and Dutch invaded North America, the indigenous people fared no better. They were hunted down and slaughtered or died of disease; those who survived were ferried into reservations or enslaved and put to work in the mines and plantations that would provision the Europeans back home or in their new lands. The doctrine of 'purity of blood', whilst explicit with the Iberians, was nonetheless inherent in the other European nations. From Alaska to Argentina, the indigenous peoples were turned into subcultures that remain to this day.

From the beginning, it became clear that the decimated indigenous population could not provide the labour necessary to exploit the wealth that was waiting to be garnered, and so the infamous Slave Trade began. This episode has been researched, discussed and illustrated to such a degree that just the mention of its name is enough to communicate the horror of what it was. However, in preparing the ground for the Industrial Revolution that followed, it played a key role. In using the human being as an animal that was disposable, maximum production at minimum cost could be achieved. The European exceptionalism and obsession with purity of blood ensured that the Blacks remained a species apart, whose only function was to labour. White indiscretions would go unacknowledged and the resultant children absorbed into the Black community. Even today President Obama, whose mother is white, is referred to as 'black'. The caste system remains.

The Industrial Revolution launched the West onto another level and made the Europeans invincible. The first machines invented were for spinning and weaving, and the North of England, with its fast-moving rivers, was the ideal environment to power the machines. But the British woollen textile manufacture could not be industrialised; the guilds were far too strong and the market fully supplied. Cotton provided the answer as it was imported from India, and Great Britain now controlled Bengal, the most important state producing cotton goods. Within a few years Bengal was turned from being the producer and exporter of the finest cotton goods to being, on the one hand, the provider of raw cotton for the mills of Manchester and, on the other, importers of its finished products. This was done by placing high tariffs on the export of cotton goods from Bengal and low tariffs on the imports from Manchester.

When it was found that the long staple cotton from North America worked better with the machines than the short staple cotton from India, cultivation of the crop was switched to the slave plantations in the Americas. Bengal was the first of many craft societies to be destroyed in order to make way for industrialisation. When the British arrived in Bengal it was famed for its wealth. Dacca was a thriving city of several hundred thousand people and, as well as textiles, Bengal was a major exporter of rice. When the British left, Bengal was a symbol of poverty, stalked by famine. A system in balance, that was locally based, self-sufficient, highly productive, stable, and working with nature, whose products were prized and sought after throughout the world, was replaced by a centrally controlled monoculture that was unstable, exploitative and worked against nature. The machines required raw materials to feed them and markets for their finished products. The British were the first to transform their trading empire to fulfil this requirement. Following the conquest of Bengal, the rest of India was brought under British control.

A large population with many cities and a country replete with natural resources became the Jewel in the Crown of the British Empire. All those crafts that could compete with British products were eliminated, including ship building, for which India had long been famous. With the introduction of the railways, the raw materials of India were linked up to the ports where they were shipped to Great Britain on British vessels, which returned with the finished products that supplied the world's largest captive market.

Whilst the 19th century belonged to the British, it also saw other European nations industrialising. To support this development, these nations either adapted their existing empires or claimed new ones. The French had lost most of their empire to the British in the 18th century and had to rebuild. Paul Doumer, French statesman and President of the Republic, stated the situation without ambiguity:

> Southeast Asia is the ideal colony, it has no end of raw materials and would serve as the perfect outlet for our factories' finished products.

And then came the moral justification:

> Just as Rome civilised the barbarians beyond its borders, we too have a duty to extend French culture and religion to the backward peoples of the world.

The conquest of what became French Indo-China (Vietnam, Cambodia and Laos) took decades. The French colonisation was always resented and resisted by a high civilisation with a deep history, which the French were unable to recognise. Just as happened in Indonesia with the Dutch, the French attempted to reclaim their colony after World War II when the Japanese had been evicted by the Americans. A ferocious war of independence followed and the French finally withdrew, only to be replaced by the Americans in their crusade against communism. The other areas of French activity were in North and West Africa, where the tragedies of Algeria and Senegal unfolded.

Russia, which had already absorbed the vast lands of Siberia, now moved south to conquer the sultanates of Central Asia and the sultanates on the northern shores of the Black Sea under Ottoman suzerainty. They now had everything they needed in one land to transform their world into an industrial giant. Italy and Germany only became nation states in the middle of the 19th century. By this time there was very little left with which to build their empires.

At the end of the century, what is known as the 'scramble for Africa' took place. Up until then, apart from North Africa, only enclaves along the vast coastline had been occupied. Now explorers and missionaries revealed the immense wealth in the interior waiting to be exploited. The Europeans decided not to fight over this, but to divide the continent up between them in a 'civilised' manner. In 1892 Bismarck, the German Chancellor, chaired a conference in Berlin to 'divide the cake', as Leopold II, King of Belgium, described the exercise. Lines were drawn on maps and the continent was cut up into countries which bore little or no relation to the tribal and historic boundaries that existed. With the invasion of Ethiopia by the Italians in 1936, only Liberia, set up by the Americans for returning slaves, remained free of European colonisation. With extreme brutality, Africa was turned into a world of mines and plantations, producing cash crops for Western markets. Once again self-sufficient societies, with their own rich cultures and living in harmony with nature, were destroyed and replaced to support the industrial system.

In the East, one nation rose up and was able to match the Europeans. Japan had closed its country to the Europeans since 1642 when the Portuguese were expelled. In 1853, Commodore Perry sailed into Tokyo harbour aboard the United States' frigate *Susquehanna* and gave the Japanese an ultimatum: either trade or else. The Japanese realised that they had to industrialise or be destroyed. They took the West as their model and selected from the different nations what they considered to be their best attributes. However, Japan had few natural resources, so it turned itself into a military/industrial nation of awesome power and acquired its own empire along European lines. By the outbreak of World War II, it was occupying Korea, a large part of China and much of South East Asia under a yoke of unspeakable cruelty and exploitation.

After World War II and its terrible nuclear end, the Japanese made what was seen to be a miraculous recovery; they became a global leader in the manufacture of many of the products that were becoming essential to the ever-changing modern way of life. However, the transformation of Japanese society brought this lament from Kenzaburo Oe, their 1994 Nobel Laureate:

> My observation is that after one hundred and twenty years of modernisation, since the opening of the country, present day Japan is split between two opposite poles of ambiguity. The way Japan had tried to build up a modern state was cataclysmic.

In other words, the Japanese have become culturally schizophrenic, living in two contradictory worlds.

The 20th century belonged to the United States of America. Born out of a colony of the British, the United States became the masters of the Americas and the most powerful nation state ever. The land from the east to the west coasts had been cleared of its inhabitants and connected by the railways, and the Mexicans had been driven out of their lands to the south. The United States now constituted a vast landmass, full of natural resources waiting to be exploited. Rapid industrialisation took place and a gulf began to emerge between the United States and Latin America.

Latin America was perfectly placed to become a United States colony in all but name, with its abundance of cash crops and raw materials and a growing market for its factory-made products. The despotic rule that had been established by the Spanish and Portuguese was perpetuated by the ruling elites that retained power in the wake of their departure, and was to continue under the direction of United States governments and corporations. It seemed that the high ideals of liberty and freedom were for home consumption, not for export. The suffering and exploitation of Latin America continued and continues still.

By the end of the 19th century, the Spanish Empire was on its last legs. Spain had lost its South and Central American colonies, but still had a number of strategically placed islands in the Atlantic, including Cuba; and in the Pacific, Guam; with one of its prized possessions, the Philippines, perfectly positioned for trade with China. Cuba and the Philippines had been in revolt against the harsh Spanish rule for years. *Noli me Tangere* is a novel by Jose Rizal which graphically describes the struggle the Filipinos were going through in their attempt to rid themselves of their tormentors. Jose Rizal was a part of the resistance and was captured and executed in 1896. His book is an amazing testament to the decadent nature of the Spanish occupation. The United States, which had been deeply critical of the Europeans and their empires, now joined them in empire building. They went to war with the Spanish and this tipped the balance. The Spanish ceded their colonies and the United States inherited a network of islands which would become, after World War II, bases for their military which would straddle the world. The Filipinos, however, had no desire to replace one master with another. They resisted and fought valiantly against the superior forces of the invader and were finally vanquished, losing 200,000 lives.

Nothing reveals more clearly how European exceptionalism was fully shared by the Americans than President McKinley's justification for the war against the Filipinos:

> We could not leave them to themselves, they were unfit for self-government and they would soon have anarchy and misrule over there, worse than Spain's was. There was nothing left for us to do but to take them all, and to educate the Filipinos, and uplift and civilise and Christianise them.

With the emergence of Germany as a sovereign state, everything was set for the final showdown of empire that would bring to an end Europe's five hundred-year hegemony. The late arrival of Germany upset the balance in Europe. Already the Prussians alone had defeated the French in the Franco-Prussian war of 1870-1871, and by the end of the 19th century a united Germany had become a powerhouse of industry, overtaking Great Britain. But there was nowhere for it to expand to support its growth. Fired by an extreme nationalism, which, after defeat in World War I morphed into Hitler's fascist state, Germany attempted to carve out its empire on European soil, turning the Slavic world into its India.

The horrors of its conquest were little different from what other European nations had committed in creating their empires, but it was done on home ground to white people, and this time the Jews suffered an industrial-scale extermination. In the end the Allies, harnessing the manpower and resources of their empires and with the support of the Americans, ended Germany's aspirations. By the end of the war Europe lay in ruins. After centuries of bloody conflict, the Europeans finally came together in a union, pledging never again to go to war against each other. But the European empires ended badly. After the war, many of the colonised still had to fight for their independence, with particular savagery meted out by the French and Dutch, whilst the British, through chronic misgovernment, left India deeply divided, which led to the partition of the country and all the horrors this entailed, the repercussions of which still haunt us. The colonisers left behind newly created, malformed nation states with traumatised citizens living in a kind of cultural limbo trying to recover their identities.

The Industrial Revolution was to give birth to a new political configuration which embroiled the world in another round of disruption and violence. The horrors of the Industrial Revolution and the exploitation of the factory workers did not go unrecorded or without attempts to alleviate their suffering. Charles Dickens brilliantly captured in his novels the atmosphere of exploitation and humiliation of the poor and the cruelty and pride of the rich. With many others in Victorian society he campaigned for reform. In the early 20th century, Charlie Chaplin brought home in his films the humanity of those living in grinding poverty under the dehumanising impact of the machine. He taught us to empathise with them, and he could do it because he himself grew up in dire poverty. There were those who believed that the capitalist system was irredeemable and simply had to be destroyed. These were the nihilists and anarchists who caused havoc for decades, assassinating a Tsar, a prime minister and many ordinary people in their bombing campaigns.

On the other hand, there were the serious political thinkers who sought an alternative solution to the organisation of industrial society, foremost amongst whom was Karl Marx. His work was the catalyst for a conflict that would engulf humanity at terrible cost, between two materialist ideologies, two sides of the same coin: capitalism and communism. Many of the leaders of the freedom movements were inspired by Marxism and espoused the communist ideal. Fidel Castro's victory in Cuba and his triumph over the Americans was an inspiration for all those nations seeking self-determination, and the downtrodden poor who were looking for liberation from despotic rulers.

The United States, having been born in a revolution against a despotic rule, that of the British, mutated into an industrial-military behemoth of unimaginable size and destructive power.

The war between the Soviet Union and the West may have been 'cold', but it was very hot elsewhere; Korea, Vietnam, the Horn of Africa, Mozambique, Columbia, Peru and Afghanistan all suffered years of conflict and there were many other flashpoints. The Soviet Union in its process of industrialisation had sacrificed its rural population to crippling episodes of famine, and to match the West had become an industrial military state. The many nations that were locked into the Soviet system were ruled with a rod of iron. The Marxist ideal had, in practice, turned into a tyranny that was brilliantly portrayed in George Orwell's *Animal Farm.*

China, the other great nation that had espoused communism, had not been colonised, but during the 19th century and deep into the 20th century had suffered grievously at the hands of both the West and Japan. From the 16th century, the beauty and sophistication of China's trade goods had attracted the Europeans. But until the Industrial Revolution, they had to trade as equal partners; China was simply too vast and strong to be colonised. With industrialisation everything changed. Along the south coast of China, the European nations claimed their enclaves, where they terrorised the Chinese into trade agreements which drained the country of its wealth. Foremost in this were the British who fought two wars to impose their trade in opium upon a people who were ravaged by the drug. A high Chinese official lamented:

> The great profit taken by the barbarian is all taken from the rightful share of China. By what right do they, in return, use a poisonous drug to injure the Chinese people?

Following in the footsteps of the Europeans was the utterly devastating Japanese occupation, which only ended with Japan's defeat at the end of World War II. This was then followed by civil war between the two Western ideologies of capitalism and communism. The communists were victorious, and Mao Zedong set about completely transforming Chinese society. More efficient in imposing atheism than the Russians, he reversed the traditional hierarchy and its connection to heaven which had for millennia nourished and renewed Chinese civilisation; in his Cultural Revolution he gutted the traditional culture, replacing it with his little Red Book; as in Russia, he sacrificed rural workers in his great leap forward into industrialisation, and as in Russia, terrible famines ensued.

Famine has always been an inevitable consequence of the changes necessary for industrialisation to take place. India had suffered famines before but nothing like the frequency and severity of those during British rule. In his book *Late Victorian Holocausts*, Mike Davis plots their courses. It has been estimated that as many as 60 million Indians may have died in policy-driven famines during the British Raj. Countless millions died in Russia and China, but only a final global count of those who suffered the most terrible of deaths to make way for industrialisation will reveal the full horror of humanity's descent into the Modern World.

China's adoption of communism brought it into direct confrontation with the United States. Becoming a nuclear power protected it from invasion, and its support of North Vietnam, with the defeat of the United States, gained China immense global prestige. In the end, the Soviet Union could not match the power of the West and fell apart, the Cold War was over and the West had won. Russia returned as a sovereign nation and the Orthodox Church re-emerged. However, China did not collapse. China's awesome craft heritage has returned in the new guise of industrial production, and China has once again become the powerhouse that it has been throughout most of history. China has been able to marry a communist regime with a capitalist market economy. Its great expansion is now fuelling global growth and Africa is once again being exploited for its vast natural resources by a new global behemoth.

The war between capitalism and communism sank the world further into the materialist mire, destroying what vestiges of traditional societies remained. The capitalist triumph ensured that it would not take more than a few decades for the modern cult to reach full maturity and become the global standard for all nations to follow.

When listing the benefits that empire delivered, those apologists for empire who want to make Britain great again place at the top of the list the rule of law. Yet nothing betrays the European delusion more completely than the idea that the cultures and civilisations that they conquered were bereft of law. Because of their idealisation of the dead worlds of Greece and Rome, they were unable to recognise, respect and relate to living worlds and so destroyed them with the belief that they contained nothing of value. Lord Macaulay expressed the attitude clearly in his *Education Memorandum* of 1823 when he wrote:

> Who could deny that a single shelf of a good European library was worth the whole native literature of India and Arabia?

In the same memorandum he spelled out the task that lay ahead:

> We must do our best to form a class of persons Indian in blood and colour, but English in tastes, in opinions, in morals and in intellect.

The power and absolute self-belief of the British carried everything before them. Once again, Lord Macaulay neatly summed it up:

> The English are the greatest and most civilised people that ever the world saw.

Such overweening arrogance allowed the British and the other European powers to impose their version of civilisation across the world. Architects were shipped from Britain to build classical government buildings and Gothic churches in Calcutta, the Malays were taught English history, the Indonesians Dutch history, the Algerians were forced to speak French, and the Brazilians built an opera house in the Amazon rainforest.

Our post-empire world has left those who were colonised full of anger and confusion, and none more so than in the world of Islam.

7

THE AGE OF CRISES

ISLAM

ISLAMIC CIVILISATION contained within itself the power of cyclical renewal, and this world of such stability, strength and sustainability could only be conquered and destroyed from a source that came from outside, and as we saw in the previous chapter, this conquest came from the West. For the world of Islam, along with all the other non-European cultures and civilisations, the Age of Crises began with this destruction. The destruction was so thorough, and the world that replaced it so alien, that Muslims were traumatised and all but lost their memory.

Nothing conveys this more vividly than what happened to Islamic architecture. In the 19th century, the Ottomans, demoralised by the apparent success of the West, abandoned their tradition, and replaced it with Western classicism. Years later, in the 1960s, a young Egyptian architect, Abdel Wahid el-Wakil, enrolled in the Architectural Department at Ain Shams University, Cairo. He wanted to study Islamic architecture. However, the course only included classical and modern architecture. Fortunately, he was introduced to Hasan Fathy, a lone figure who was single-handedly recovering the principles of the tradition. In the 1980s el-Wakil would realize these principles in a series of mosques of surpassing beauty. A dozen edifices were erected in Saudi Arabia over a decade, including the rebuilding of the Quba Mosque, the first mosque to have been built in Islam.

Those Islamic lands colonised by Europeans had not only their architectural traditions but their entire cultures, to a greater or lesser extent, replaced by European models. Islam in India suffered a terrible destruction after the rebellion of 1857; the Muslim intelligentsia was decimated and the higher education system destroyed, leaving a dangerous vacuum. Those nations that remained independent, as we have seen, carried out the process of destruction upon themselves. With the collapse of Islamic civilisation, the synthesis that had brought together all the branches of knowledge in the contemplation of divine unity, fragmented. In this fragmentation, various possible approaches were separately expressed and the mereological principle was breached, with each tendency claiming for itself the whole truth. For example, 'Salafi' literalists have remained with the face value of the Scripture, mirroring the Protestant Reformation with their abandonment of the historic tradition and return to the source, while the neo-Muʿtazilite rationalists, now under the spell of modern science, have imposed their rationalist interpretations on the Revelation. Both tendencies deny the validity of Sufism, and, without the protection of the hierarchy of knowledge, true Sufism has become vulnerable and been made to appear extraneous to Islam.

This destruction of a world that had been so successful and dominant for a millennium, led the traumatised Muslims to ask the question: how could this have happened? The most natural response was for Muslims to blame themselves. They had failed God, and God was punishing them. A trap was forming that would imprison the Muslim mind. Muslims could decry the moral decay that they could see taking place in the West, however, they were transfixed by the power of modern science. The myth that developed as part of the narrative of progress was appropriated by the Muslims: during Europe's Dark Ages, Islam had made a major contribution to the development of modern science; without the Muslim contribution, the European Renaissance could not have taken place;

after their 'Golden Age', the Muslims had declined, stagnated, fallen asleep, become all mystical; now they must wake up and catch up. The marriage between Islam and modern science became the great quest, one that has engaged and is still engaging the Muslim intelligentsia. It is a quest that is impossible of realisation, modern science having emerged out of the materialist mindset that has broken the balance and produced the Age of Crisis.

We can see three stages which the cultures and civilisations of the world went through when faced with the irresistible power of the West. At first, they fought to defend their lands. In the second stage, once the land had been conquered, the people mostly submitted to their new rulers, with sporadic outbreaks of rebellion taking place and being ruthlessly crushed. The third stage is absorption into the Western system, or being left as an impoverished remnant. The absorption was achieved through the adoption of the sovereign nation state, Western education, and the power of modern science.

The power of modern science first made its impression through military warfare. As states conformed to the new reality, the doors were opened to Western experts and specialists, who brought in their wake the whole modern package. Those nations that were not colonised, enacted upon themselves the process of westernisation. Above we saw what happened to Japan. The Ottoman Empire followed the same course. In the Ottoman Empire, the process went in stages: during the 19th century Western military experts came, and this was followed by a reformation of the education system and the codification of law. As we related above, the Ottoman sultans were so demoralised by the success of the West that they vacated their traditional palace and built a classical palace, in imitation of Versailles, nearly bankrupting the State. With their defeat in World War I, wholesale modernisation and westernisation took place, and the Ottoman Empire was reduced to the Turkish nation state. With this, the breakup of Dār al-Islām was complete.

The fragmentation of Islamic civilisation has produced tyrannous nation states, and nation states that have descended into complete chaos. The symbiosis between farmers and nomads has been broken by modern agribusiness, leading to terrible conflict and massacres, such as in Darfur and across the Sahel. Young Muslims, assailed by the seeming success of the West and the chaos within Islam, are deeply confused and many are losing their faith. Zealous atheists are targeting them. Richard Dawkins, their high priest, is having his books translated into Arabic, Persian and Urdu, and made freely available. Another trend is the attempt to bring Islam into compliance with modernity; ever-changing modernity becomes the criterion by which to judge Islam. And the judgement often focuses on aberrational and criminal behaviour by Muslims that is, in fact, a rejection of Islamic values.

All the traditional cultures and civilisations that were destroyed to make way for the modern world were reduced to chaos, conflict, confusion, civil strife and violence. However, the response to their destruction was mostly contained within their national borders, with the exception of Islam; since it has no national borders, the response has been and continues to be global, and of a scale and intensity exceeding all those that have gone before; the greater the unity, balance and stability of an entity, the greater will be the chaos, confusion, conflict and violence in its shattering. All shades of human response are taking place within the Muslim *umma*, from serenity, compassion and patience, to anger, violence and criminality.

Among demoralised Muslims, witnessing the persecution and suffering of their fellow Muslims across the world, the phenomenon known as the Ghost Dance has surfaced. This originated with the Plains Indians of North America at the time when they were reduced to complete hopelessness. A saviour appeared bringing a message of hope and salvation; through the enactment of a particular dance, the ancestors would reappear and an army would sweep away the white man, the buffaloes would come back and everything would return to what it had been before the arrival of the white man. This rebellion, which spread across the Great Plains, marked the final tragic uprising of the Plains Indians. The phenomenon also inspired what is known as the Boxer Rebellion in China and precipitated the last major act of resistance to the European plunder of the Celestial Empire. With the Muslims, the same phenomenon has emerged in the vain attempt to recreate the Caliphate; an act so full of delusion, anger and revenge that it has transgressed every principle of the religion it claims to represent and has turned Islam in the eyes of the world into its opposite, to the horror and despair of most believing Muslims.

And yet Islam continues to grow throughout the world. The universal appeal of Islam is still alive. The Revelation speaks to all humanity and, as we have seen, was translated into a successful civilisation. The Muslim is at home in the world, he and she are truly global citizens. At this time, when all humanity is wracked by instability, suffering and fear, many Muslims, surrounded by a world in crisis, are finding inspiration and solace in the thirteen years of trials that the Prophet endured in Mecca, and are attempting to follow his example by responding with patience, forbearance, compassion and love for humanity and for His creation. For the sacred core of Islam remains intact and fully operative. Just as Islam was completely manifested in the time of the Prophet, and in its formation as a universal civilization, so it is perfectly formed as a haven from the storm that humanity is now passing through.

THE WEST

THE AGE OF CRISES has been a long time in the making and we have followed its trajectory from the collapse of Western Christendom until the storm that now encompasses us. What we have witnessed in each of the chapters of this book is not an ascent but a descent, from intense spirituality through humanism to an all-encompassing materialism. In Chapter One, it was from the sovereignty of God to the sovereignty of the individual; in Chapter Two, from a God-centred society governed by obligations, to a human-centred society asserting its rights; in Chapter Three, from religious contemplatives seeking to understand God's purpose, to modern scientists attempting to understand how the material world came into existence and what it is made of; in Chapter Four, from Christian ascetic to modern consumer; in Chapter Five, from the sublime beauty of the cathedral to the chaos and ugliness of modern art; in Chapter Six, from Western Christendom on the edge of the civilised world, to world conquest by the reborn 'civilised' West, and to the West's creation of the Modern World. Finally, in this chapter we arrive at the Age of Crises. At the root of this downward trajectory is the breakdown of Christendom. Once the walls were breached, there was nothing to arrest the ever-increasing descent into materiality, which is now spiralling out of control, and which has produced a world and way of life that is far from the ideals of Christianity.

Our Age of Crises is the culmination of what is being described by the British Geological Survey as a new geological era:

> Humans are now drivers of environmental change on a scale that is unique in Earth's history. Human-driven biological, chemical and physical changes to the Earth's system are so great, rapid and distinct that they may characterize an entirely new era – the Anthropocene.

With the splitting of the atom and the dropping of the bomb, humanity for the first time had within its power the capacity to destroy itself. Over the last seventy years that power has multiplied, following the chthonic principle that the deeper you delve into matter, the greater the forces that are released. With the ever-growing release of powers within the material realm, the crises have escalated and a once benign natural world is turning hostile and unpredictable.

The meta-narrative which gave purpose to the Western world has fractured. Societies are divided. The middle ground of liberal democracy is failing.

Artificial Intelligence is gradually taking over an increasing range of human occupations. The gulf between rich and poor is widening. Debt is mounting, and it is becoming increasingly difficult to maintain the modern way of life. Politicians are appealing to past glory, nationalism and fear of the outsider in their attempts to revive societies.

But arguably the greatest danger is that the failure of modernity has given birth to a philosophy that threatens a complete breakdown of society. Postmodernism has entered the mainstream of the West and is disintegrating the social order; complementarity in human relationships has been replaced by uniformity; the sovereignty, liberty and human rights of the individual are now enshrined in a philosophy that has reduced everything to relativity. The love and inclusivity which is its justification, expresses a profound desire for a wholeness and integrity of which, ironically, it is the antithesis. All that holds the current fragmentation together is the dynamic of economic growth. Once this falters nothing will be left. But incredibly, the idea of progress is so powerful that it has managed to subsume postmodernism, which spells its demise, into its narrative.

The West first attempted to impose Christianity, then its version of civilisation and then modernity on the rest of the world. And now, in what must be the last act of Western exceptionalism, the West is attempting to impose post-modernism upon humanity.

However, there is still a great reservoir of compassion and thoughtfulness in the West. There is generosity in response to the crises taking place around the world, and many have devoted their lives to alleviating the suffering of those affected. Deep thought is being invested in trying to understand what is happening, and to find a better way of living sustainably on earth. Many are recognising the wisdom contained within pre-modern cultures, and are seeking to preserve, practise and promote traditional husbandry, health and knowledge systems. The awareness of the abyss facing humanity and the desire to retreat from the edge is growing day by day, as news of the escalating crises reaches every corner of the globe.

CONCLUSION

HOW HAS OUR UNDERSTANDING of Islam and the West been affected by changing our perspective from progress to balance? Essentially, the situations have been reversed; whereas in the narrative of progress, the Western arc was one of ascension and the Islamic arc one of stagnation and decline, in the new narrative Islam maintained the balance whilst the West broke it, descending ever more rapidly into the realm of materiality.

For Muslims, their story ceases to be one of failure. Islamic civilisation provided an intellectual and environmental framework in which peace was achievable through all of life's vocations. The Islamic principle of *mīzān*, in all its meanings of balance, equity and justice, was at the heart of this world and remains the bedrock of the religion. Islamic civilisation had a remarkable capacity for cyclical renewal and, as we have seen, its destruction had to come from an outside power. Now the Muslims are suffering the shattering of their world. But they are not alone; all the traditional cultures and civilisations had to be destroyed to make way for the modern world, and the first to be destroyed was Western Christendom itself.

From the perspective of balance, the unreality of the modern West becomes clear. With the breaching of the mereological and chthonic principles, the balance was upset, and an aberrational world came into existence which is releasing ever greater powers of destruction.

However, the warnings from within the West, and especially England, have echoed through the centuries. Marlowe's Dr Faustus sells his soul to the devil in exchange for mastery over the intelligible universe; Marcellus in *Hamlet* declaims that 'something is rotten in the state of Denmark'; Milton's paradise is lost; Blake's 'dark satanic mills' are destroying the spirituality of 'this green and pleasant land'; Wordsworth describes how 'Men, maidens, youths, mothers and little children, boys and girls,' enter these new satanic 'temples' and are offered up as 'perpetual sacrifice' … 'To Gain, the master idol of the realm'; and as a premonition of the terrible future of the new sciences, Mary Shelley creates Frankenstein's monster.

As we enter the 20th century, the warnings continue; for TS Eliot we are turning our souls and the world into a 'Wasteland', and the Irish poet Yeats sums up the chaos gathering between the world wars at the beginning of his poem 'The Second Coming':

> Things fall apart; the centre cannot hold;
> Mere anarchy is loosed upon the world.
> The blood-dimmed tide is loosed, and everywhere
> The ceremony of innocence is drowned;
> The best lack all conviction, while the worst
> Are full of passionate intensity.

For the dystopic vision of the future we are bringing upon ourselves, we have *Brave New World* by Aldous Huxley and George Orwell's *Nineteen Eighty-Four*.

In England, where the Industrial Revolution was born, there has been a constant desire to return to a past when communities were at home with nature and when the church and cathedral were at the centre of village and town life. Many people and movements have carried on the battle to preserve and restore our traditional environment and way of life in face of the ever-increasing encroachment of modernity: William Cobbett in his writings and campaigning; Pugin with the revival of Gothic architecture, and the Oxford movement with the restoration of the Catholic tradition; John Ruskin and William Morris in their attempt to recover craftsmanship and beauty in the face of factory-made products; and the many attempts at returning to the land and farming in a manner that is in harmony with nature.

The beauty of our traditional environment and the buildings erected to the glory and worship of God are a constant reminder of the centrality of religion to our way of life through most of our history. This held true until the recent decades when the modern cult fully manifested itself and gave birth to the Age of Crises.

GLOSSARY OF KEY TERMS

Mīzān – An Arabic term which can be translated as balance, justice, measure, harmony or weighing scales. It is a term which contains a spiritual dimension that is not conveyed by our secular understanding of balance. It is the lens through which this study has been made.

Mereological Principle – 'the whole can contain the part, but the part cannot contain the whole'. This is a fundamental principle that has been developed in this study. It is essential in understanding the nature of unity and universality, and the aberrations that occur when the part claims to be the whole.

Chthonic Principle – 'The deeper you go into matter, the greater the forces that are released'. This is another fundamental principle that has been developed in this study.

Ontological Triad – The relationships between the heavenly, human and material domains.

Vocational Triad – Priests & Scholars, Warriors & Statesmen, Merchants & Craftsmen; these are the key categories whose relationships determine the character and dynamic of civilisations.

Platonic Triad - Plato formulated the principle of the need to balance three faculties within the human being, namely, those of Intellect, Anger and Desire, a principle that was adopted and developed by both Christianity and Islam.

Dynamic Equilibrium - I have introduced the term 'dynamic equilibrium', which comes from the material sciences and is defined as 'a state of balance between continuing processes,' or 'a system in a steady state', to describe the dynamic which maintains the *mīzān* or balance.

Idealisation of a Dead World – The Renaissance idealisation of the Greco-Roman world, a world that had been dead and buried for a thousand years. This resulted in the European becoming a detached observer, and the separation of religion and culture.

Dialysis of the Imagination – the dependence on a machine-delivered source of entertainment that takes over the imagination and produces an addictive state.

Normalising the Abnormal – Humanity is used to living in a state where fundamental norms exist. The modern cult requires the normalisation of the abnormal for its existence.

Modern Fallacy – The idea that humanity has been delivered from a past of misery, poverty and stagnation into the light of the modern age.

Modern Cult – I have likened the modern world to a cult because, as the historian Christopher Dawson observed, modern man is cut off from both the heavens and the earth. Modernity only makes sense in terms of its own criteria and is out of step with reality.

A LIFE'S JOURNEY
THE STORY BEHIND A BOOK

A Life's Journey is the companion volume to *Rethinking Islam and the West,* and tells the intriguing story behind Keeler's challenging thesis.

In this book, Ahmed Paul Keeler recounts an extraordinary life that began in the 1940s with an idyllic childhood in a conservative Christian family in Windsor, and continued with the trauma of an English boarding school education intended to prepare him for running a British Empire that, by the time he left, no longer existed. Life then took him through three years of drama school and the angst of modern theatre, five years' involvement with the cutting edge of modern art, an immersion in the 60s counterculture and then, through a series of life-changing encounters, led him to embrace Islam.

A born organizer, Keeler was producing plays as a teenager, and in his 20s set up and ran the pioneering Signals Gallery which promoted kinetic art. However, on another scale altogether was his creation of the World of Islam Festival of 1976. Opened by Her Majesty the Queen, this was the largest and most comprehensive cultural event of its kind ever to have taken place in London. Following this success,

Keeler initiated and was engaged with various projects relating to Islamic civilization, traditional culture and the environment, the greening of inner cities and the interaction between cultures and civilizations in the pre-industrial age.

At the age of 70, Keeler finally yielded to a friend's insistence that he should make available to others the knowledge he had gained from such a rich life, by writing a book. The result was *Rethinking Islam and the West: a New Narrative for the Age of Crises*, a work which questions the modern world's obsession with progress, and proposes that the true criterion for judging the success of a civilization should be that of *mīzān* or balance. This principle makes it possible to see the history of Islam and the West in an entirely new light.

A LIFE'S JOURNEY

THE STORY BEHIND A BOOK

Ahmed Paul Keeler

ISBN: 978-1-9161738-3-5

EQUILIBRA

Printed in Great Britain
by Amazon

50639020R00108